HERMANN HESSE
Phoenix Arising

By Paideia Publishing Company

Stephen Leacock
Arcadian Adventures with the Idle Rich
Stephen Leacock
The Unsolved Riddle of Social Justice
Ron Dart
Hermann Hesse: Phoenix Arising

Paideia Publishing Company

Published in 2019 by Paidiea Publishing
Abbotsford, BC, Canada
Copyright © 2019 Ron Dart

Dart, Ron
Hermann Hesse: Phoenix Arising

ISBN: 9781706249351
Edited by T.S. Wilson
www.paideia-publishing.com

PHOENIX ARISING
Ron Dart

CONTENT

INTRODUCTION

"Unlike his great contemporary, Thomas Mann, Hesse has no power to bring people to life; but his ideas are far more alive than Mann's, perhaps, because Mann is always the detached spectator, while Hesse is always a thinly disguised participant in his novels. The consequence is that Hesse's novels of ideas have a vitality that can only be compared to Dostoevsky; the ideas are a passion; he writes in the grip of a need to solve his own life's problems by seeing them on paper."
Colin Wilson *The Outsider*

"America witnessed a Hesse phenomenon that was unparalleled for a European writer."
Paul Morris

"When New Directions decided to publish the first English translation of Hermann Hesse's Siddhartha in 1951, it could not have foreseen the enormous impact it would have on American culture."
Paul Morris

"Considered as a whole, Hesse's achievements can hardly be matched in modern literature; it is the continually rising trajectory of an idea, the fundamental religious idea of how to 'live more abundantly'. Hesse has little imagination in the sense that Shakespeare or Tolstoy can be said to have imagination, but his ideas have a vitality that more than makes up for it. Before all, he is a novelist who used the novel to explore the problem: what should we do with our lives?"

Colin Wilson *The Outsider*

The fate of Hermann Hesse (1877-1962) within the literary, political, religious and philosophic fashion shows has, predictably, waxed and waned, waned and waxed. We seem to be, these years, in a waxing phase of Hermann Hesse. In short, Hesse is very much a phoenix arising yet again.

I think we can note six seasons of Hesse being on and off stage in the larger cultural ethos of the 20th and 21st centuries. The first phase was Hesse emerging as an avante garde German writer with distinctive romantic leanings in the late 19th and early 20th centuries. The poetry of longing and unique sensitivities could not be missed, but his initial breakthrough novel, *Peter Camenzind* (1904), placed Hesse at the forefront of a new generation of German writers. The publication of *Beneath the Wheel* (1906), *Gertrud* (1910) and *Rosshalde* (1914) made it abundantly clear Hesse could live the vocation of a writer. The second phase made for a worrisome road bump. WWI emerged, and Hesse was no patriotic German. In fact, he dared to question the aggressive German tendencies that brought WWI into being and many a fan turned on him for his lack of committed nationalism. These were not easy years to live through---Hesse was maligned, caricatured and opposed, sales on his writings thinned out. In WW1 Germany needed committed and uncritical nationalists and Hesse was not that. The end of WWI and the suffering of those who lived through it made many receptive to writers with more internal probes. *Demian* (1919), *Siddhartha* (1922) and *Steppenwolf* (1927), although veering in different directions for diverse reasons, pondered the complex and layered nature of the psychological paths taken, dependent on what part of the inner life was listened to and why. In the 1920s Hesse was very much on his literary feet again in Germany and Europe. In this the third phase of his life-- dark clouds were on the horizon, Hesse read their message well, he had left Germany, was living in Switzerland, and the future was unclear and uncertain. But, for the most part, Hesse was virtually unknown in North America. As WWII became a reality Hesse published many a superb short story, poem and book, including *Journey to the East* (1932) and his epic classic, *The Glass Bead Game* (1943), the final full flowering and abundant fruit on the tree of his life. The Nobel Prize in Literature was awarded to Hesse in 1946.

The 1946 Nobel Prize in Literature ushered Hesse, slowly yet significantly, into the fourth phase of his life journey and literary migration to North America. By the 1950s, the post WWII reality of North America was one in which a counter culture was slowly emerging that questioned American imperialism, injustices of civil rights, the Vietnam War, an education system that lacked soul, a form of secularism that undermined spirituality, emerging ecological concerns and deeper probes into the human soul. Hesse's many books were, increasingly so, published in English, and Hesse became, in some ways, a must-read rite of passage author (one of the few European writers) in the counter culture of the 1950s-1960s-1970s. It can be legitimately questioned whether Hesse's status as a North American cultural icon was a result of a thoughtful and mature read. Nevertheless, Hesse became, for many, one with the European and North American counter culture of the decades shortly after WWII—such was then the fourth phase of Hesse's life, his actual literary output in the 1950s, leaner than in previous decades.

With the thinning out of the high noon of the counter culture in the latter decades of the 20th century Hesse's life and writings waned. In this fifth phase of Hesse's writings, he had become so identified with the earlier ethos of the counter-culture, that with its passing he also passed out of sight and seemed to be no more. Other than as a cultural artifact and museum piece of an earlier era, Hesse was rarely taught in German literature classes in the 1980s-1990s and the early years of the 21st century. We are now, though, living in the sixth phase of Hesse's reception. Gratefully so, a more mature read of Hesse has occurred in the last 10-15 years. Hesse has become delinked from the more immature read of him in the counter culture decades, and a fuller, more mature and nuanced read of Hesse is before us. It is to this fuller and more comprehensive approach to Hesse (and his perennial relevance) that this book is dedicated.

It is pertinent to note that there is much more to Hesse than his evocative and challenging novels. There is his wide ranging wisdom poetry that is embodied, for example, in *The Seasons of the Soul: The Poetic Guidance and Spiritual Wisdom of Hermann Hesse* (2011) and *Hymn to Old Age* (2011). There are also the thousands of letters Hesse wrote, including the must read correspondence between Hesse and Thomas Mann and Roman Rolland. And, there is Hesse the voluminous painter, a book yet needed that delves much further and deeper into his sensitive landscape palette. There is, of course, Hesse's many short stories and Fairy Tales as embodied in *The Fairy Tales of Hermann Hesse* (1995), *Strange News from another Star and Other Stories* (1972) and *Stories of Five Decades* (1976). There are also the many biographies of

Hesse and his reflective and pictorial autobiographies. And, true to his more political and war-peace concerns, his many essays from 1914-1948 in *If the War Goes On....* (1971). I might also add that some of Hesse's other reflections on the larger Tolstoyan themes of war-peace such as "A Dream About the Gods", "Strange News from Another Planet", "If the War Continues", "The European" and "The Empire" can be found in *The Fairy Tales of Hermann Hesse* (Translated/Introduced by Jack Zipes).

Needless to say, there are many portals to enter the highly creative life of Hesse, and in this book I will ponder the ongoing relevance of Hesse from a variety of perspectives. First, I will touch on some of Hesse's earliest published writings in which we can get a sense of his emerging and yet still immature reflections: *Peter Camenzind* and *Kulp-Wanderer* will hold our attention at this point. Second, we will focus on some of Hesse's deeper probes in his spiritual quest and how such a quest has played itself out in the past and potential present: *Siddhartha* and *The Journey to the East* are two must reads in this genre. Third, we will turn to Hesse's summa and most comprehensive and demanding tome of a philosophic and cultural beauty: *The Glass Bead Game*. This is a book that asks of the reader many a read and reread---there is so much pondered and reflected upon in this updated version of sorts of Plato's *Republic* and *Laws*, the Castalians being the new philosopher kings and Joseph Knecht (Magister Ludi's dilemma) snared between the intellectual and contemplative life in tension with the active and productive life. Fourth, we will engage in some comparisons and contrasts with other thinkers that either had an impact on Hesse or who Hesse impacted: "Burckhardt-Nietzsche-Hesse", "Hesse-Merton" and "Erasmus- Heidegger-Nietzsche-Hesse" will bring to a close the more comparative articles.

Martin Heidegger spoke, amongst many things, of our "thrownness". We are all thrown into a period of time in which the significance of religion, politics, arts and culture, ecological issues, the contest and struggle to define the good life and human identity, and much else is brought to the dock and part interpretive paths as ideologues wage war with one another. Our ethos is one in which an understanding of western civilization is being questioned, pondered, caricatured and interrogated in heated culture wars. Who has thought deeply about these issues, who can we heed and learn from, what are the differences between right and left reads of "The Great Tradition?"

The obstinate fact that in our thrownness we dwell in an age of excessive "memoricide" yet further complicates the issues of understanding — where there is no substantive memory of the past, cultural, political and religious pathfinding is hard to do. Hermann Hesse gave most of his life to thinking and living these issues, hence this primer and key in the ignition book about him. May his sensitive insights guide us through the darkness, turbulent waves to a blue sky, port and home.

I might also add, by way of a succinct ending to this introduction, that Hesse's deeper vision of the new being and person of meaningful depth and integrity can best be found, in a chronological order, from Peter Camenzind (and his attraction to Francis of Assisi), Siddhartha, Narcissus (and such a wise rethinking and redefining of the metaphor) to Leo in *The Journey to the East* and finally to Joseph Knecht in *The Glass Bead Game*. There is an obvious sense that as Hesse points to these overcomers the more convoluted inner and outer lives described in *Demian* and *Steppenwolf* are left behind and Hesse becomes the 20th century sage of wisdom, insight and love.

I suppose, in this book on Hesse, I should note that I have sat with and read Hesse's books, short stories, poems and fairy tales for many a decade, and I have been most fortunate to have spent lingering time at his home in Montagnola in southern Switzerland (near the border of Italy).

I have also spent some enjoyable time at Nietzsche's home in Sils Maria in the Engadine Valley in Switzerland. I have thoroughly enjoyed walking the many trails Nietzsche did and sitting at the sites where he often sat. Hesse, more than most in his generation, engaged Nietzsche in a sensitive and probing way--- hopefully, this book will reflect how this was done and many other probes Hesse made into

some of the more difficult issues of the human
journey.

amor vincit omnia
Ron Dart

1

PETER CAMENZIND

There and Back Again

"In the beginning was the myth."
1st sentence *Peter Camenzind*

When they had finished eating, Jesus said to Simon Peter, "Simon son of John, do you truly love me more than these?" "Yes, Lord", he said, "you know that I love you". Jesus said, "Feed my lambs".
John 21: 15

The publication of Hesse`s *Peter Camenzind* in 1904 was, in many ways, Hesse`s breakthrough novel. Hesse had published a few minor works of poetry and literature before 1904, but with the publication of *Peter*

Camenzind, Hesse became more widely recognized as an up and coming German writer. Many know Hesse today, at a more sophisticated level, as the author of *The Glass Bead Game* (*Siddhartha* being the primer for the larger tome that, in some ways, won him the Nobel Prize for literature in 1946). But, there are many other compact novels that have held the attention of Hesse keeners: *Demian, Steppenwolf, Narcissus and Goldmund, Under the Wheel, Wandering, Gertrude, Rosshalde* and *If the War Goes On…* (to include his more political writings). There is also Hesse`s volumes of poetry, multiple paintings and thousands of letters. Hesse, like Thomas Mann, embodies the best and the highest of the German humanist way that has many a thick root going back to the layered soil of Goethe's life and writings.

It is somewhat intriguing that Hesse engaged Nietzsche in many subtle and sensitive ways and yet Nietzsche is very much in the ascendant these days and waxing well, whereas Hesse (much wiser and more insightful) has waned. There has been, gratefully so, in the last decade plus, a revival and renaissance of Hesse, and, as such, a return to Hesse`s *Peter Camenzind* is a fine place to begin a journey with Hesse into the core of what animated his soul and mind, imagination and literary life.

Peter Camenzind is a short novel written in a most lyrical and poetic manner. It is the unfolding tale of Peter`s journey to what truly matters in his (and our) all too short trek through time. Many was the bypath and detour taken by Peter from his early years in an isolated Alpine village (where the scenery is described by Hesse in mesmerizing detail), death of a dear friend (Richard), failed relationships that once held much hope and promise (Rosi, Ermina & Elizabeth), tangled family upbringing, a substantive experience in a more aesthetic high culture of literature, painting and music — there is also an affinity with St. Francis, an ongoing attempt to parse the Nietzsche-Francis challenge, his attentive compassion to both Agnes (who died all too young), the hunchback and social outcast Boppi and a return to his alpine home village (Nimikon), as the there and back again tale comes to a close. But, there is much more to the drama than this hasty overview. Let us ponder the beauty and allure of this timely life journey.

Why did Hesse choose the title he did for this poetic pilgrimage novel of sorts? Why Peter and why Camenzind? The Camenzind natural yarn and silk company was started in Switzerland (near the Rigi Mountain range) in 1730. There is a sense in which the life of Peter is like the delicacy of fine silk and yarn being spun into the garment of his soul. The task of the human journey, being both like silk and yarn knit into a literal and metaphorical garment, cannot be missed as a metaphor and portal into the novel. And, why Peter? The fact that the missive is set within Germany, Switzerland and Italy speaks volumes, plus Peter's interest in

Roman Catholicism and St. Francis. Peter is a doorway into the journey similar to St. Peter (not necessarily in context, content and deed but certainly in principle), the vicar of Christ in Rome. The original Peter (disciple of Christ) made many a gaff and roundabout on his pathway to his final vocation and charism — the pilgrimage of Peter Camenzind is no different. So, this updated parable of sorts into how a meaningful life might be lived is already hinted at in the title of the book.

The presence of the warm yet powerful alpine wind (*Fohn*) broods over the initial chapter of the novel. The *Fohn-Foehn* confronts the snow and winter, mountains and rock-hard ridges, stirring avalanches, heralding spring life in the mountains, communities and soul. It is this ongoing natural phenomenon that can also be found in societies along the human journey. There is order and predictability, security and stability, and such order can create a closure to the deeper changes and transformations that might occur in the life journey. The *Fohn-Foehn* brings a shift in the seasons, points to warmer weather and the vast array of alpine flowers---it is both greeted and feared, welcomed and opposed (as if fear and opposition will halt the life-giving winds). It does not take too much reflection to ponder the relationship of the alpine spring wind and the reality of the Spirit. It is such a wind that brings changes, and Peter's insulated life in Nimikon is about to be altered.

Peter's youthful yet somewhat protected life in Nimikon takes him out of all he has known into the larger world of schooling, education, cities and a more bohemian artistic ethos and life style. He is introduced via his friend, Richard, to a vast array of artists who see themselves on the cutting edge of the inner and outer life pilgrimage. Needless to say, Peter feels quite intimidated by such a tribe, given his more rural and mountain upbringing where he never experienced a real sense of higher culture, literature and education seen as of only minimal importance. The simple tasks of mountain survival were the alpha and omega of village life in the high alpine.

A significant part of *Peter Camenzind* deals with this journey from a shire life of sorts into the larger world of thinking and the arts, culture and the cultivation of the more refined and sophisticated life. Peter is, initially, drawn into the wonder and appeal, allure and possibilities of such a way of being. Increasingly so, he comes to see such a way of being as somewhat higher and more significant than the herd in the valley and villages of life. Such a way of seeing makes him separate himself from the common life. This leads, in time, to isolation, loneliness, and too much drinking. There is a sense in which Peter had been quite taken by the challenge of Nietzsche and was attempting to live forth such a philosophy. There was also the world of Nature and St. Francis and, also, the more communal intellectual life and soirees in Basel that Peter was drawn to (in some ways the Jacob Burckhardtian (1818-1897) challenge to Nietzsche (1844-1900), Richard Wagner (1813-1883) being an anathema to both).

The larger and more urbane intellectual life that Peter attempted to parse (trying this, trying that) was offset by his many rambles and longer treks in the mountains, along old mountain trails, resting in such places, body and soul more at peace and rest. The views and vistas seen, the body exercise, the peasants met on the pathways also spoke to Peter about something deeper, hardier, and more at one with Nature and community life. Again and again, the exquisite description of mountain scenes by Hesse border on the musical and poetic. There comes a place in the journey for Peter when Nature becomes the antidote and healing balm to an overly intellectualized urban life. But, Nature cannot answer the deeper need for human friendships and community, and Peter becomes acutely aware of this nagging dilemma.

The more Peter ponders his inner and unfulfilled longings and desires (Nature not being an adequate answer and antidote to loneliness and isolation), the more he is drawn to Italy and the Umbrian countryside (where St. Francis was active). Peter temporarily settles into an Italian village where he befriends many children, the larger community and an adoring lady. There is a growing sense in which Peter, at this point in his journey, is much more committed to a Franciscan life: simplicity, community, brother sun, sister moon, children. But, this Umbrian community is not his home, although his experience in it alerts him to a more meaningful path worth the taking.

Peter makes a difficult decision to return to his home village to see how his aging father is doing. There are multiple touching scenes in this part of the book—his father's weakening state, his attempts to support his father even though father and son are quite different—the village he grew up in not truly knowing the nature of his journey, and his many returning memories of relationships that never truly matured into desired hopes and dreams. Life does go on but memories of what might have been ever linger and haunt.

The final chapter in this beauty of an instructive primer on the deeper and more committed life comes as an affront to our highly mobile, transient and individualist liberal culture and ethos. Peter has travelled much terrain (inward and outward) in the novel. He has come to see that a simple life style, close to nature and in community (vow of stability of sorts) nourished his soul in places the other options simply did not. The novel ends with Peter returning to his home village and parish of Nimikon in the high alps, not regretting what he has seen or been, but aware through experience that life in an older and time tried parish does more to connect and knit together than idealistic wandering in search of meaning, or a naïve thinking that the aesthetic and artistic life can slake the thirst and hunger for deeper meaning or purpose. Peter has come to see, by novel's end, as did St. Benedict centuries earlier, that faithfulness to community (never easy when tensions and clashes emerge) and commitment to place and people will do more to deepen and transform the soul than many of the alluring alternatives.

There is a sense in which Hesse through the character of Peter is suggesting that quiet service (a feeding of the sheep) in community is the more significant myth worth internalizing and living forth in a world that is divided, fragmented and often shallow and superficial, chasing one distraction and amusement after another, ever restless but never at peace or ease. The theme of kindly and faithful service as embodied in Peter can be found in many other of Hesse's later novels: *Siddharta, The Journey to the East* and *The Glass Bead Game,* the finale of the mythic vision. Jesus had to ask Peter three times if he loved him, given Peter's erratic and questionable behaviour. It was natural that Peter questioned his faithfulness to Jesus, but Jesus affirmed, again and again, Peter's potential. The test, by day's end, was whether Peter could overcome his doubts and fears, his sense of betrayal and inadequacies, and simply and faithfully, feed and nourish the community. Such was the education of Peter Camenzind. Such was the place that the *Fohn-Foehn* wind unfroze and softened him, such was the nature

of both the delicate silk and natural yarn woven,
as a garment onto Peter's soul.

2

KNULP AND WANDERING
The Bohemian Phase

esse had established himself, as a compelling and attractive writer, before WWI. The publication of such Hesse classics and primers as *Peter Camenzind, Under the Wheel, Gertrude, From India, The Prodigy* and *Rosshalde* placed Hesse at the forefront of a thoughtful and emerging German and European romantic tradition and ethos. But, dark clouds were emerging at a variety of levels in Hesse's life: WWI and tensions at home with wife and family were demanding their exacting due. Hesse saw all too keenly, given his sensitive temperament, the imposing challenges before him. It is understandable, from a certain perspective, why the need for a certain escape from such growing responsibilities can and might occur. When life becomes too overwhelming, there is a tendency to go to places where the sky is clear blue, there are no dark clouds, and much is calm and peaceful----such is, in some ways, the naively sweet, yet worth the read, *Knulp* and *Wandering*.

Ralph Freedman suggests that in *Knulp* Hesse "developed the figure of the perennial wanderer--literally the sensitive hobo-who could stand out as the vagabond *par excellence* (p. 140). In many ways, *Knulp* anticipates some of the American Beat writers that emerged after WWII, Kerouac's *On the Road,* for example, a decade's later version, athough perhaps, not as tender and elusive as *Knulp.* There is a definite sense in which Hesse in *Knulp* is pondering both the appeal and end destination of those who are ever on the road, uprooted and committed to nothing other than the next step of being on the trail of life. The 3-part life story of Knulp tracks and traces his life from that of a seemingly gifted person, his departure from what he might have been if he had continued his schooling, painful and disappointing life experiences, his longing for a home and settling but never making the decision to do so.

Knulp was published in 1915 and is divided into three sections or tales: 1) Early Spring, 2) My Recollections of Knulp 3) The End. Needless to say, the young Knulp of the early spring phase, has a winsome, winning and delightful charm to him. He has turned aside from the expected demands in his life and has chosen to live as he wishes and wants—there is a spring like budding and blossoming in this tale but also consequences of making such decisions and living them out. The young Knulp appeals to the child within and what Blake might call the "songs of innocence".

The next section of the short story walks the interested reader into the "songs of experience", life demanding its inevitable due and exacting wage. While "My Recollections of Knulp" takes the reader to Knulp in midlife stride, Knulp now living into the troubling reality of his earlier decisions made. The midlife phase tends to be more layered and complex, the fresh and bountiful scenery fruit and air of "Early Spring" now fading into Knulp's summer and emerging autumn years. "The End" brings Knulp's final years to a conclusion. Alone and deserted, assistance from an old doctor friend initially received, Knulp takes to the road again and dies penniless, snow frozen and starving, the temptation of the early spring season, once absolutized and made a vocation, ending in a tragic and painful way.

Who has not seen Knulp's life in their own life? Hesse certainly understood the temptation, and poignantly described the end journey of those who make a vocation of ever wandering, committed to nothing but wandering.

There is a sense in which *Wandering* is a companion missive to *Knulp,* although the end is not so sad and sobering. *Wandering*, unlike *Knulp*, is a series of short reflections and sketches of a wanderer who makes a walking pilgrimage from Switzerland, over an alpine pass, and into Italy, WWI now over. Each short reflection and poem ponders significant life issues in a tender and probing way. The short book begins with the wanderer leaving what he has known and been, and heading southward alone to the lure of Italy (a common European and German literary destination). The wanderer is ever the outsider, watching and observing, yet ever moving on. The final chapter, "Evenings", like *Knulp*, portrays the wanderer, like a spectator in a play, watching the drama of life but refusing to be committed to act on the stage. The wanderer, therefore, is torn between longing for some sort of meaningful life, a commitment to place and people, and yet refusing to make the decision that will ground him. Ever the reflective and uncommitted skeptic, impotent and paralyzed in the maze of his insights. *Wandering* was published in 1920, Hesse was feeling the brunt of many a German nationalist having turned on him, the literary elite being suspicious of him, his marriage ailing, his children with friends and relatives, his life, in many ways, in a turbulent and painful place. The wanderer, like Knulp, remains the lone romantic individual, unheard and misunderstood by the bourgeois, philistinian, and thoughtless classes of the time.

Hesse's question, of which *Knulp* and *Wanderer* were provisional answers, was this: how is the sensitive artist and political oppositional thinker to respond to opposition, indifference and those close to the bone relationships unravelling? Is the answer to isolate oneself, leaving society and family behind, committed to observing the unpredictable, and much ado about nothing in much of life? Idealism once betrayed can and often does lead to cynicism or a form of realism in which life is hard and painful, hence only by being alone and isolated can one avoid being hurt and betrayed again. And yet such a stance of indifference and skepticism creates its own difficult dilemmas. Those who retreat into their private worlds of inner reflection and, at times, meaningful insights, but disconnect themselves from other people and community, predictably so, often become depressed and disoriented, solipsism and nihilism their tempting companions on the journey. Hesse has certainly probed such a path hiked in these two small books (worth many a read), but his deeper and more mature thinking and writing goes further and is more nuanced than *Knulp* and *Wandering*. It is to these more thoughtful novels we now turn to see Hesse ever growing in his nuanced probes on the journey of life.

It is probably of some significance to note that twenty-two of Hesse's fairy stories written between 1904-1918 were edited and published by Jack Zipes, as *The Complete Fairy Tales of Hermann Hesse* (1995). The shorter and earlier version was published in 1919 in German as *Strange News from Another Star* (translated into English in 1972). Many of these fairy tales highlight the trying and difficult nature of growing into wisdom, depth and maturity. It is in this sense that the fairy tales are a companion and corrective to what might seem to be the rather thin and subtly indulgent life journey embodied in *Knulp* and *Wandering*, the life of the detached wanderer and bohemian. A thorough immersion in the fairy tales will reveal a meditative breadth and depth in Hesse's life and writings not necessarily discovered in *Knulp-Wandering*.

3

SIDDHARTHA
Ferryman Servant and Wisdom

"When New Directions decided to publish the first English translation of Hermann Hesse's Siddhartha in 1951, it could never have foreseen the enormous impact it would have on American culture."
Paul Morris (p. xiii)

"Hinduism has been much misunderstood in the West since it has been introduced in one or another of its exaggerated forms. One image of it is that of the starving sannyasin who by dint of extravagant austerities claims to have realized himself as the soul of the All....The other is that of a religion of unbridled sexuality which the publication of the Kamasutras as a paperback has done nothing to dispel."
R.C. Zaehner *Concordant Discord* (p. 163)

"American witnessed a Hesse phenomenon that was unparalleled for a European writer."
Paul Morris (p. xv)

There has been and continues to be in our post-Christendom, post-secular scientific Western culture and ethos a perennial spiritual longing and thirst that only deeper waters can quench. The West has a significant contemplative tradition as does the East. Kipling wrongfully suggested that "East is East and West is West and never the twain shall meet". There have been many creative writers and thinkers in the last few centuries that, in our increasing global village, have sought to discern, how East and West might meaningfully meet — Hermann Hesse is certainly such a guide and mentor, one who in his layered and longer life, sought to bring together the wisdom and contemplative traditions of the West and East: *Siddhartha* was one of Hesse's fuller forays into such thoughtful probes.

For the more sensitive and thoughtful, the sheer carnage and tragedy of WWI raised questions about human suffering on our all too human journey. What does it mean to be human and live an authentic life? What decisions aren't worth making, and how can we be deflected from making such decisions? Is there more to being human than the fleeting ego, throes of matter and projected public personas?

It was these sorts of questions that greeted Hesse and demanded a response. Hesse's apparant turn to Buddhism as an initial attempt to face such questions after WWI was not, it should be noted, a scholarly and academic approach to examining the origins and sources of the emergence of Buddhism---Hesse's interest was much more existential and personal. Hence, the Siddhartha of this short novella is not the Siddhartha turned Gotama Buddha (the enlightened one) of 1st generation Buddhism — it is much more the story of every person who longs to live a more meaningful life (and the hard decisions that point in such a direction).

Siddhartha is divided into two parts, Part One being much shorter than Part Two, although Part One sets the context and stage for Part Two. Hesse began writing Part One shortly after WWI in 1919 and finished the shorter text in 1920---the missive was published in 1921. Part One contains four compelling chapters: The Brahmin's Son, With the Shramanas, Gotama and Awakening.

The main mythic theme of the deeper life journey is developed in part one---Siddhartha and his friend Govinda are raised with the elite religious leaders of the day, Siddhartha's father being a Brahman, faithful adherence to the holy texts, rites, rituals and sacred religious forms, the mark of a genuine Hindu spiritual leader. And yet, Siddhartha had a deep aching emptiness within that the historic and establishment religious forms failed to soothe or transform. The weaning from both his father/mother and his hunger for more than what was offered by the Brahmanic tradition and ethos led Siddhartha and Govinda (his faithful friend) to the lean ascetics (With the Shramanas). Would fasting, begging, chanting and hours of meditation still, expose and reveal the ever-illusive ego? How could Siddhartha live consistently from the eternal atman within? The external rituals of the Brahmans and the internal demands and disciplines of the Shramanas (Siddhartha and Govinda were with the ascetics for three years) still did not clarify for Siddhartha the deeper transformative places he longed to live from. Govinda mentioned to Siddhartha that the Gotama Buddha was an enlightened one they should visit and so they did. Gotama had, obviously, reached a place of deep inner peace and poise---his followers were growing in abundance. Govinda decided to stay with Gotama and his disciples. Siddhartha, after a brief meeting with Gotama, was taken by his obvious integrity of character, but he realized, he would never live from a deeper place by simply becoming an uncritical devotee of Gotama. And, so the journey of awakening began.

Part One ended with Siddhartha knowing what he had to leave behind, knowing what he needed to be free from but unsure of what he was to be free for. Such were Hesse's conclusions in 1920-1921. Hesse had to go to deeper places in his life journey before the larger and more mature book *Siddhartha* would be birthed from his soul and creative pen. The quote from Zaehner from which I began this essay speaks much about one notion of Hinduism---"that of the starving *sannyasin* who by dint of extravagant austerities claims to have realized himself as the soul of the All". The fact that the young Siddhartha was the son of a Brahman, joined the ascetic Shramanas and met Gotama the Buddha speaks much about a certain read of Hinduism-Buddhism. But, there is much more to the unfolding journey into releasing the skin encapsulated ego than such an inward spiritual turn---such was the position of awakening that ended Part One of the book. Part Two walks the reader into the much longer and more nuanced journey of the maturing Siddhartha.

Zaehner mentioned that the other distorted and extreme read of Hinduism was "that of a religion of unbridled sexuality which the publication of the *Kamasutras* as a paperback has done nothing to dispel". The latter part of Part One and the initiation into Part Two, makes the move from a form of spirituality that attempts to transcend matter, history, flux and transience of both nature and human nature and dwell within the eternal atman that is Brahman. Such a move walks the aspirant beyond the temptations of nature, matter, the flesh, sensuality, sexuality, the senses and the lures and baits of the fleeting and transient. This detachment from such deceptive attachments is the mark of the authentic spiritual pilgrim---such is the *sannyasin*. But, the dilemma is this---Siddhartha was still in the grips and prison of the ego and a certain reactionary dualism that denied matter (in its various forms and guises) as a means of enlightenment.

Between Part One and Part Two Hesse lived through a sort of dark night of the soul in which he had to go deeper into his layered and undealt with inner life and emerge with more mature insights — the fact he was a directee of sorts of a Jungian psychologist (later working with Jung himself) meant Hesse had to probe many of the deeper archetypes and myths of the soul in a way that he had not substantively done until this season of his unfolding life. Hesse began a return to the novella in 1922 and by October 1922 *Siddhartha* was complete. What then is the deeper wisdom and insights of Part Two that make this missive such a book of perennial interest?

Part Two walks the reader into the world of time, the senses, physical appetites, and life in the world. The young Siddhartha, having shed his ascetic robes, enters the city and meets, Kamala, the alluring and seductive courtesan. Kamala, in time, teaches Siddhartha all the delights and charms of sex (all so abhorrent to the ascetics). Kamala also introduces Siddhartha to the wealthy businessman, Kamaswami. The world of the senses, business, wealth and opulence soon take possession of Siddhartha and he indulges many a desire and longing that would have seemed unthinkable in his former life. But, the deeper Siddhartha delves into such an ethos (and does exceedingly well in it), the more he realizes, he is less and less happy, more and more soul desperate. He has, in short, everything at one level but nothing at a deeper

level. He is, in fact, like a dying bird in a cage---
such was a dream he had that woke him from
his soul dying slumber. The world of the "child
people" who only lived for the senses,
sensuality, wealth, possessions, property,
amusements and a diversity of distractions was
the world of samsara, the wheel that goes round
and round and never ends. How to get off the
wheel of samsara and go to deeper places again
became the relentless question of the now aging
and forty year old Siddhartha. His was a similar
tale to Solomon in *Ecclesiastes*. Siddhartha had
played the illusive game of samsara and done
well at it, but was now tired of such mirage
mongering. It was time to leave the world of the
"child people", their mindless addiction to
samsara and enter the third phase of his ever-
deepening journey — such is the portal into the
chapter called "By the River".

Siddhartha had lived the ascetic and
sensualist lives, both forms in which the ego
holds its way and sway, the water of time
washing him and cleansing him, past lives
disappearing down the river of time. The
ferryman at the river's edge (Siddhartha had
met him before as he crossed over from ascetic
to sensualist) greeted him yet again. The image,
of course, of crossing over, of leaving the
shoreline of one way of life to the shoreline of
another is rich with symbol---such was
Siddhartha's next phase of the journey in which
he met Vasudeva, the aged and aging ferryman.

The deeper lesson Siddhartha was yet to learn was the passage of learning to love, of being attached, of being knit to another, of not being aloof, detached and the perpetual observer---such had been his way as the Brahman's son, his time with the shramanas and his time with Gotama (and his disciples including Govinda). But, his life with Kamala, Kamaswami and all his earthly successes was also about a sort of game playing, acting a role, still detached and the perennial watcher. Siddhartha was aware "he had been unable to love anything or anybody" (93) — such was his tragic and sad fate. How was he to overcome such a dilemma and narrative? In some significant ways these were Hesse's questions at this stage of his life. Even though Siddhartha had scorned the "child people" he came to realize he was just a more sophisticated version of them---deception does take many different inner forms, some being more subtle than cruder and more obvious versions and temptations.

There are a few refrains in *Siddhartha* that recur again and again — there is a listening to the classical inner "daemon", a heeding and hearing "the bird in your breast", the "secret voice", harkening to the child within and learning to be silent and listen, listen and listen yet ever more maturely, authentically and accurately. Such are the more meaningful spiritual disciplines Siddhartha had yet to learn, and it was the ferryman, Vasudeva, that would become Siddhartha's final teacher and mentor. There is a fallacious tendency to think that because Siddhartha is the main actor in the book that Hesse was leaning more in the direction of Buddhism than Hinduism. Although, I don't think this is the case. It is significant to note that both Vasudeva and Govinda (Siddhartha's teacher as the ferryman and his longtime friend) are both, in their different ways, connected to Krishna (8th avatar of Vishnu). Vasudeva is sometimes viewed as the earthly father of Krishna or identified with Krishna. Govinda has many an affinity with Krishna, Krishna in the Puranas, Gita and Mahabharata is the god of bhakti love, the lover of the loved. There is, in Hesse's choice of Vasudeva and Govinda, (given their connections to Krishna) a substantive relationship to the lover-loved mystical tradition of India that can be found in a variety of Indian traditions. This is all quite different than the early form of Buddhism of Gotama that factors in *Siddhartha*.

Who then are Vasudeva and Govinda and why are they so significant in Siddhartha's maturing transformation? Vasudeva is very much the elder to the younger and somewhat still confused Siddhartha. Vasudeva has sat by the river, spent years listening to its life-giving message, learned to be internally still, centred and at peace. Siddhartha, when he has left the city, has much in him that is at war, much needed to confess. Siddhartha has led a life in which he has, essentially, trusted no-one, been close to no-one. He left his father when young, left the ascetics, his friend Govinda joined Gotama, his relationship with Kamala and Kamaswami (the former nearer and dearer than the latter) somewhat detached. Vasudeva had the maturity to simply wait and allow Siddhartha to share of his deepest human pain and confess his multiple confusions and inner aloneness---it was like a frozen waterfall thawing then cascading fresh and life-giving water. As Siddhartha says about Vasudeva, "Few people know how to listen, and I never met anyone who knows how as well as you. In this, too, I will learn from you" (104). It is this stance of attentive listening that Vasudeva teaches Siddhartha much about himself and a deep friendship of trust emerges and matures. The two men come to be known as the sages by the river. But, this short season in which Siddhartha seems to have found an inner peace is soon to be challenged. History is to catch up with him.

Gotama is near death and many who have been his disciples and devotees are making their pilgrimages to be with him in his last days. Much to the surprise of Siddhartha, Kamala has left her job as a courtesan, given all her wealth and possessions away and is en route to see the dying Gotama — her son is with her, her son, the child of her final night in bed with Siddhartha. There is a touching scene in which Siddhartha and Kamala momentarily see one another and become one at a longing level, but Kamala has been bitten by a serpent and dies in the arms of

Siddhartha. This means that Siddhartha and Vasudeva inherit the petulant and spoiled son of Siddhartha and Kamala. The chapter, "The Son", takes Siddhartha to places in his life in which his son opposes, defies, rejects and delights in causing great pain to his father. How is Siddhartha to respond to his son? Should he, in kindness and gentleness embrace such behavior, hoping in time a change will come? What happens when his son grows increasingly angry and defiant, rude and oppositional? Needless to say, much sadness and grief enters the heart of Siddhartha. Vasudeva suggests to Siddhartha that there comes a time, hard as it is, that he must release his son. This is painful for Siddhartha for the simple reason that he has slowly learned what it means to love, to be attached, to be knit together with another---in this case his son. And, now the sadness of attachment works its way out via his final moments, the death of Kamala and his angry and reactionary son. Kamala had once told Siddhartha, "you are incapable of love---he had agreed with her and had compared himself to a star and the child people to falling leaves" (120). Now, he was learning the meaning of listening love and the predictable suffering it caused. Should he be the aloof and cold star again? He had come too far to return to such a place in his soul.

The moment came in which Siddhartha's son erupted in anger with his father and left the riverside and returned to the city of shallow delights and transient amusements. Siddhartha knew at one level he had to let his son go and yet his emotions spoke a deeper and more demanding message. Siddhartha yet once again revealed his deep soul pain to the ever listening and attentive Vasudeva who understood the layered dilemma. How does one hold together attachment and detachment in a wise and discerning manner? It is much easier to be naively attached or glacial like detached. Siddhartha followed his son to the city but knew he would have to bear the beams of love with no resolution or final happy ending. It was inevitable that Siddhartha would return to the river to be with Vasudeva, Vasudeva ever the attentive listener who heard the deeper message of the river and Siddhartha's anguish. Siddhartha, like the river and Vasudeva, soon came to see all things in their comings and goings; decisions and consequences flowing like a river ever in motion, new seasons of life emerging as old are washed away. This was a higher wisdom then the world of Brahmans, ascetics and Gotama---this was a deeper way of seeing and being than the game world of samsara.

The final two chapters in the book, "Om" and "Govinda", bring the tale of Siddhartha to a close. Vasudeva, in time, knows he must die and die he does. Siddhartha becomes the ferryman who takes, at various levels, literal and spiritual, those who must cross the river, from one shoreline to the next. Some merely see the river as a place to cross as quickly as possible. Others hear the river and know in the crossing much can be heard and seen. The more the destination dominates, the less the ability to see the wisdom of the river crossing process. Govinda, the old friend of Siddhartha, makes a final visit to the river not realizing, in his haste and goal setting ways, his friend was the ferryman. There is final reflection by Siddhartha about seeking, love and listening in the final few pages of the book that Govinda hears but does not hear---he moves on, planning to cross the river, his restlessness unabated, the journey to his friend's inner peace and stability not understood. "Love, for me, Govinda, is clearly the main thing" (144). This tends to be Siddhartha's final summary before an almost transfiguration scene occurs as Siddhartha kisses Govinda on the forehead. The scene illuminates much and draws forth from the depths of Govinda's deeper but often repressed longings. The final paragraph needs to be quoted in full to get a sense of what Siddhartha had become and what Govinda might yet become.

> "Govinda bowed low. Tears of which he was unaware ran down his aged face. A feeling of most profound love and most humble veneration burned like a fire in his heart. He bowed low, down to the ground, before the motionless, sitting figure whose smile reminded him of everything he had ever loved in his life, of everything in his life that had ever been worthy and sacred for him."

WHAT is Hesse saying with such a poignant and graphic, raw and tender ending? There are a few things to note by way of conclusion. First, the Siddhartha of the novel is not the Gotama Buddha of Buddhism — Siddhartha comes to his awakening not through some enlightened teacher but through a deeper listening to the inner voice that is affirmed by the unnoticed yet wise ferryman Vasudeva. In short, insight, if ears and soul are attentive, can often be found by some of the most ignored yet thoughtful people rather than charismatic leaders. Vasudeva had lingering time for Siddhartha in a way Gotama Buddha never could or would with his many uncritical devotees. Second, it was not by sacred texts, rituals, asceticism, the play of ideas or indulging shallow appetites that Siddhartha found his way---it was much more through a deeper listening, attentiveness, kindly mentoring, searching inner sensitivity and friendship that Siddhartha learned an inner peace. Third, if love was the final message of the novella, then love is higher than knowledge and wisdom, and love is more about growing in attachment and oneness with others (as painful as this can be a times) than aloofness and detachment — it is also about seeing the transient and passing not as something to be avoided and transcended but as a very icon of seeing deeper.

After seeing who Siddhartha truly was did Govinda remain with him, just as Siddhartha learned from the river and Vasudeva? Such an answer is not given us but we do know Hesse has offered in *Siddhartha* many significant and wise insights into human nature, its distortions and aberrations, its possibilities and the need to discern paths of meaning rather than paths of mis-meaning and poor route taking — and yet, much can be learned from questionable paths taken. As Shakespeare noted, "by misdirections we find direction out".

Hesse had emerged in German literature in the early part of the 20th century with the publication of *Peter Camenzind* (1904). He had published earlier works of poetry, prose and book reviews but by 1904, Hesse was being noticed more and more as a rising literary star. *Beneath the Wheel* (1906), *Gertrud* (1910) and *Rosshalde* (1914) consolidated his reputation as an on the cutting-edge German writer and creative thinker. The coming of WWI, though, put Hesse in a precarious place. Hesse was no uncritical fan or booster of German nationalism and the aggressive nature of Germany. The articles he wrote between 1914-1918 that questioned German nationalism meant that many who once cheered him on and were boosters for his literary career began to turn on him seeing him as a traitor to the German people, state and nation. Needless to say, such opposition and marginalization cut deep into Hesse's soul. The multilayered novel that brought Hesse back to public prominence was *Demian* (1919). *Demian* is a rite of passage book for the young Emil Sinclair in which light and darkness, shadows and shade, misreads, wise insights and the notion of ultimate being (the mythic god Abraxis) good and evil mix and mingle in the chalice of the book. There can be no doubt in *Demian* that Hesse is feeling his way along some treacherous and unsure pathways. The publication of *Siddhartha* needs to be seen in such a context. There is a simple clarity, rinsed eyes beauty and cleaner road walked in *Siddhartha* than *Demian*. Both books need to be read together to get an obvious sense of Hesse's transition from a rather confused spirituality to a more focused and centred vision of our all too human journey.

The Siddhartha of *Siddhartha* is the wise sage who, in a servant like manner, ferries one and all across the waters from shorelines of leaving to shorelines of new transitions in life. Siddhartha has lived through much, seen much, suffered much, loved much and from such an immersion in life, he is both kindly, merciful and ever the aging ferryman.

The novel does end very much with an individualistic answer to the journey, but many of the more time tried perspectives anticipate Narziss in *Narziss and Goldmund*, Leo in *Journey to the East* and Joseph Knecht (Magister Ludi) in *Glass Bead Game*. Narziss summed up his understanding of the deeper and more substantive life by saying, "The goal is this: always to place myself there where I can best serve…Within that which is best possible to me, I will serve the spirit as I understand it". The movement from the more individualist oriented spiritual journey to the more communal monastic of the League in *Journey to the East* and yet fuller community of the Castalian in *The Glass Bead Game* highlights an obvious maturation in Hesse's vision of the more substantive journey. The issue of servanthood and quiet service often underwrites how a community of depth, at the highest life, should co-inhere. Leo, for example, is the oft invisible yet servant like leader of the League (only recognized for who he truly is at the end of the book) just as Joseph Knecht is the Magister and servant like leader of the more sophisticated Castalians. There is, in short, an obvious progression in Hesse's thinking and life in regards to his idea of the authentic life, servanthood, community and leadership— Siddhartha is but the initial pointer in such a maturing direction.

Hesse, throughout much of his creative and literary life, grappled with the challenges posed by Friedrich Nietzsche and his notion of the *ubermensch* and new being, Zarathustra being the prototype and model. There is a sense in which Hesse's Siddhartha, Narziss, Leo and Joseph Knecht are Hesse's quite different version and vision of the authentic Zarathustrian overcomer, but this is an essay for another time. The dialogue of sorts between Nietzsche and Hesse, Zarathustra and Siddhartha-Narziss-Leo-Knecht is a significant crossroads on the western cultural, intellectual, spiritual and civilizational pathway. Much hinges on what route is chosen and why.

4

JOURNEY TO THE EAST
Wisdom Widens

"The law ordains that it shall be so'. 'The law?' I asked curiously. 'Which law is that, Leo?' 'It is the law of service. He who wishes to live long must serve, but he who wishes to rule does not live long."
Book 1: Leo

Hesse was one of the most conscious spiritual seekers in his time and one of the finest and most consistent European doves in an age of two world wars and an ethos of overt hawkishness and militarism. Hesse fled Germany to Switzerland because of his opposition to German aggression in WWI, and his many poignant anti-war writings were collected and summed up in *If the War Goes On*.

Hesse settled in Montagnola (near Lugano in the Italian part of Switzerland) and he won the Nobel Prize for Literature in 1946 for his classic and probing novel *The Glass Bead Game*. My wife (Karin) and I had the good fortune of spending time at Hesse's home/museum in Montagnola in June 2012. It is 50 years in 2012 since Hesse died, and there is a variety of events celebrating Hesse's prolific and committed life being put on in various parts of Europe in 2012.

In the 1960s-1970s Hesse became an iconic literary guide in North America. Many in the counter culture at the time avidly read Hesse with growing interest. Hesse provided much in-depth insight on the spiritual journey at a time that many in the more secular age failed to do and many of a more religious bent lacked the ability to do. Hesse has often been wildly misinterpreted to serve diverse ideological agendas, but when read in a meditative way and manner he still has much to offer the earnest and seeking pilgrim.

At first glance *The Journey to the East* seems to be about the turn by westerners to the East for insight, illumination and enlightenment. There is a standard and typical tradition of those in the West turning against the West and idealizing the East. Was this what Hesse was doing in *The Journey to the East?* Hesse was much too subtle a thinker and wise spiritual guide to slip into the tendency to romanticize the East and demonize the West. The East is a metaphor in this tract for the times for something much deeper and more substantive. If the East does not mean the literal East, what does it mean then?

The Journey to the East is set within the context of the 20th century in which Christian states had bullied, fought and gone to war---was this what Christianity was about?----the Great War, millions of deaths and a mindless nationalism in which brothers and sisters of the same faith viciously turned on one another because of race and ethnicity. Hesse was more than aware that when nationalism and statehood trumps the deeper truths of the spirit and mind, the richness and fullness of humanity shrinks to a barbaric level. *The Journey to the East,* therefore, is more about a journey to the motherlode of what it means to be human and humane---a vision of a higher humanity that transcends the tribalism of a mindless nationalism. The backdrop and landscape to this spiritual allegory is the tragedy of the war of all against all—when such a reality exists, the higher vision of the unity of the spirit becomes demoted and banished.

The 'East' in this novella is about the League which draws together people from various times, places and cultures who know the future of humanity consists in those who are alert and aware to the real spiritual issues of human longing. The League brings together men and women who have drawn from the riches of both East and West the time tried gold from the best of their inherited traditions. All in the League are on a journey to deeper meaning. But what does Hesse mean by the East if it is a metaphor for a higher spiritual vision of human unity?

If the journey is towards the East (the Home of Light) and those in the League are committed to such a journey, what is meant by such a turn? Novalis sums it up well: 'Where are we always going? Always home!'. Or again, 'For our goal was not only the East, or rather the East was not only a country and something geographical, but it was the home and youth of the soul, it was everywhere and nowhere, it was the union of all times'. Those in the League (of whom the author of the booklet was one) were in search of the homeland of the soul that transcended both nationalism and religions. In short, the East is merely a metaphor for "the home and youth of the soul" and "the union of all times"---the East is not about a place but about the orientation of the soul towards wisdom, insight and the light.

The League existed in *The Journey to the East* as a unified group in search of such a higher truth, but as the novella unfolds, frictions emerge as one of the servants, Leo, leaves the group. Leo appears in Book I not as the leader of the League, but as a quiet and contented servant to the group. There were the Masters in the League, there were the novices and there were the servants to the Masters and Novices: Leo was but a servant. Animals were drawn to Leo (this should be a clue to the attentive reader), and he had an attractiveness about him that was most winsome and winning, but most in the

League only saw Leo as their faithful and dutiful servant who did as expected.

Leo disappears from the League in Book II, and with the passing of Leo, the League begins to have internal problems. Members begin to differ and divide on how the Ancient ways are to be interpreted, and, in time, those who were once close and united about the meaning and purpose of the League and the East part paths and go in different directions. The League seems to be, for all intents and purposes, dead and a thing of the faded past. Now that the League seems over and done, the author of *The Journey to the East* commits himself to write about the League and the journey. The painful task of writing about the eclipsed League raises all sorts of questions for the author---it seemed so solid, it was period of his life when all seemed so meaningful and focussed-----what had happened? Why did the League and Journey seem to have dissolved and the author left a spiritual orphan?

The author in Book III knows he must write about the League (it was so important at a strategic part of his life), and he knows Leo's parting has something to do with what he thinks is the passing of the League. A sort of despair has settled into the author's life (the euphoric phase seems over and the League that once gave life seems gone and done). The author is warned to forget about Leo and get on with the history of the League as a cathartic experience of sorts. The writing of history, of course, is a step removed from the living of history, but when the living seems tepid and thin, a history of lived memories offers a vicarious sense of meaning.

The years pass and the author does his best to retrieve old and faded stories in documents as he cobbles together what he can of the League. The journey seems over, but is it? Does the League still exist, and, if so, can it yet be found? Leo will not leave the author's mind and imagination. Decades have passed, and hope is strained, but the thin thread of hope persists. Book IV deals with the rediscovery by the author of Leo (who seems an older man now and quite uninterested in the League and the Journey). In fact, Leo seems almost aloof and distant when confronted by the author about the League. The one connection with the past seems futile and doubly painful. But, the author persists with his questions, and Leo relents and asks him to join him for a slow journey through the streets.

Book V brings the tale to a close. The author discovers that the League still exists. It was not the League that had vanished but the author who had failed to understand why the League existed. It was the author who left the League not the League who left the author. Leo the servant and seeming enemy of the League appears as the 'head of the whole League'. Who would have guessed that Leo, the servant, who seemed to have deserted the League, was in fact the Pope of the League? Leo's true role was only revealed at the end when the author's eyes and soul were cleansed. Until then, Leo was but a romanticized servant or challenging nemesis. It was only as the author persisted with his questions that the real meaning of the journey to the East made sense.

If the East in the novella is a metaphor for home, then the homeland of the soul, as embodied in Leo, is the life of quiet service. Leo, the true Master, was the servant of all the Novices and Masters. Only those with eyes to see the true nature of what is the real home of the soul could see Leo for who he was as the servant Master of the League. Leo, of course, is also the metaphor of the lion who rules through kindness and service rather than through dominance, power and control. Hesse had a great fondness for Francis of Assisi (he even wrote a book on Francis when younger), and Leo was Francis' true servant, companion and soul friend.

There is yet a deeper sense in which Leo, the Lion, has much to do with the Servant Christ who came not to be served but to serve. The paradox is that the wild and undomesticated lion becomes truly noble when such power is turned not to destruction and dominance but service and kindness.

What then is *The Journey to the East* about? It is not about idealizing the Orient and denigrating the West. It is about pointing the way to where the soul must go to find rest and peace. Is such a path defined by political or religious Masters and Novices who dominate others or control them through fear? Or, is it about a quiet Leo like service, discipline of the passions and longing for a higher and greater good? Leo had faced many a demon and dark night of the soul to reach his place as leader of the League. The author had now to make such a journey---so must we---such is the perennial parable and lesson of *The Journey to the East.*

5

JOURNEY TO THE EAST
The League and Leo

"Hesse's two works of these crucial years —
Journey to the East composed in 1930 and *The
Glass Bead Game,* written between 1931 and
1942 — were deeply political books in a sense
quite different from the previous novels."
**Ralph Freedman *Hermann Hesse: Pilgrim of
Crises: A Biography* p. 339**

There has been, gratefully so, a Phoenix-like resurrection in the last decade in the life and writings of Hermann Hesse. Hesse was, in many ways, a rite of passage must read author in the counter-culture of the late 1950s-1960s-1970s. Sadly so, he was, mostly, misread by those who misunderstood his layered inward and outer journey as a writer steeped in the best of the European literary and cultural, religious and political ethos and tradition. As the counter-culture of the mid-20th century moved on, Hesse seemed to disappear with it, his fate and future too linked with such a period of history. But, a more mature, subtle and sophisticated read of Hesse is afoot these days, and as such a return to Hesse occurs, much gold is to be mined in his perennial insights and wisdom.

I have been fortunate to spend time at Hesse's home in Montagnola in southern Switzerland and have lingered long with his writings and sensitive yet troubled life journey. The title of the book, in some ways, misrepresents the content of the book. Many who merely read the title falsely assume that the book is about a journey to the East in a spiritual way as a counterpoint to the decadent and unspiritual west. There is an unfortunate and somewhat superficial approach by many on a conscious contemplative journey to idealize and romanticize various types of Oriental religions and spirituality and caricature Western culture as secular, too beholden to science and religiously agnostic, atheistic or superficially religious (lacking a contemplative and meditative depth). This means that a journey to the east must be taken to recover and rediscover what is longed for at the centre and fount of the soul and spirit. But, Hesse, was much too bright and wise to slip into such a simplistic dualism and either-or approach to the religious crises of our age and ethos. How might we read *The*

Journey to the East in its context and for our troubled times? There are five points I want to briefly mention as pointers into understanding this superb classic of a book.

First, *The Journey to the East* was written and published in the early 1930s and, as such, nationalism was very much on the rise in Germany (Hesse had strong German connections but he consciously chose to live in neutral Switzerland). The rising nationalism in Germany in the late 1920s-1930s held the attention and hearts of many Germans. The notion of a people regaining and recovering their damaged reputation in the midst of both economic depression and the failure of capitalism and communism motivated many. It is in this context that significant leadership in the church (certainly not the best or all) linked the fate of the church with National Socialism — the state and religion had a symbiotic relationship. It is essential to note, though, many were the German Christians that opposed such a dysfunctional relationship. Hesse was acutely aware of such a reality and, in many ways, *The Journey to the East,* is a political rebuttal to such a notion, his vision of "The League" upping the spiritual and political ideal to a higher and more demanding unity than nationhood or race, the "Great War" ever the backdrop to this novel.

Second, how did Hesse deal with the two types of communities that confronted him at the time? If the German race and nation was an option that held many and became an absolute centre of commitment, were there higher ideals that transcended such a questionable vision? The League of spiritual searchers, as I mentioned above, brought together men and women (past and present) who acted as countervailing thinkers and activists, beacons of inspiring light and life that would not be taken captive by the blood and race ethos of the time. Most of those on such a quest in the League had a symbiotic relationship of sorts with those in the past who lived well and wisely — they were, in many ways, icons and mentors to the searchers, teachers who stood in opposition to Hitler and tribe. Some of the names and times Hesse mentions in *The Journey to the East* are unknown and foreign to most readers, but this speaks much about the literary and cultural illiteracy of our age and ethos, memoricide a dominant disease we live with. But, for Hesse (and others), such names and times offered an alternate vision to live by, a counter-culture to heed and live into. Who did Hesse point to as a model contra the *wille zur macht* of the 1930s?

Third, the narrator of the novel begins his journey and continues such a quest in a utopian community of sorts, the League consciously committed to living a deeper and more meaningful faith journey, heeding and hearing the best and wisest from history and diverse faith traditions, the "Great War" as mentioned above the ominous canvas on which this beauty of a text was painted. But, in time, the League fragments and dissipates. The main protagonist in the tale reflects back on such a significant phase in his journey and wonders why and how such a thing occurred, the best of intentions deteriorating into failed hopes and dreams, despair his growing companion. It seems, as the novel unfolds, the age of innocence now past, the age of experience pointing in two directions: cynicism and despair or the quest for deeper insight, wisdom the guiding light. It is significant to note that for Hesse the East is, in a deeper sense, the "Home of Light" and "towards home". This is the challenge of the narrator----which internal and external voices will he listen to and why? Is there a commonwealth of spirituality and virtues that transcend time, place, space, race and nation? Such a question is very much with us these days as peoples and borders are being drawn to keep foreigners out.

Fourth, the north star in the novel is Leo. The League was held together, for the most part, when Leo, the seemingly innocuous servant, was present. Most in the League ignored Leo even though they appreciated his quiet, consistent and servant like commitment to those on the quest. The animals saw Leo for who he truly was but, the irony of the tale, was those who seemed to be the most conscious in their quest did not see the deeper meaning of their journey, Leo, servant-like, in their midst. Hesse had written, earlier in his life, a short biography of St. Francis and Francis figures prominently, in his first successful novel, *Peter Camenzind*.

Hesse, being the poet and myth embodier that he was, tapped into the significance of Leo both as Francis' dearest friend and supporter and the myth of Leo the Lion (passions and strength transformed into generous service and kindness). When Leo slipped away from the League, its deeper meaning vanished and the spiritual questers lost their ability to both remain together and find their way. Obviously, in such insights, Hesse is speaking much about the deeper meaning of spirituality, politics and identity. The narrator of the novel discovers, as his journey matures that, in fact, Leo is the head of the League and, as such, clarifies the more significant meaning of the East (light, home, rising of the sun and day).

Fifth, Hesse in *The Journey to the East* was questioning and undermining the political ethos of the time with a vastly different understanding of community and leadership (spiritual insights of the best of history and religious traditions an antidote to nationalism, blood and race-----a reality very much with us again today). Hesse was also engaging, at a deeper level, probably, a thinker he had grappled with most of his life: Nietzsche. It is virtually impossible to read Hesse's novels without Nietzsche appearing on front stage again and again. Leo, of course, can be the powerful lion whose will shapes and makes the world, who dominates and faces into the tragic and, again and again, wills an overcoming of sorts. It is significant to note that the lion is at the beginning of *Thus Spoke*

Zarathustra in "On the Three Metamorphoses". Hesse's Leo as model and mentor of the new being is an alternate to Nietzsche's Zarathustra. Hesse was, of course, not only dealing with the obvious political turmoil of the 1930s but he also saw beyond such a period of time, the issue of "identity" and "human nature" in the West would become a contested issue----Leo or Zarathustra? Which and why? It is somewhat interesting that Nietzsche has held court for many a decade but Hesse has been ignored and yet Hesse is, probably, when understood aright, one of the best and finest dialogue partners of Nietzsche. Those who are seriously interested in a thoughtful engagement with Nietzsche do need to immerse themselves in Hesse's lifelong dialogue and dance with Nietzsche.

The Journey to the East is, therefore, a counter political novel to both the overt nationalism of the 1930s in Germany and Europe (offering a higher ethic) in which identity is defined by political power (and who has it) and an emerging notion of personal power in which identity, Nietzsche style, is about making and willing into reality, in a creative and constructive manner, against much cultural opposition and odds, the self-creating new being. Hesse offered, in his many novels, from *Peter Camenzind* to *Siddhartha* to *The Journey to the East* and culminating in *The Glass Bead Game* the notion of the self as a kindly and thoughtful servant of civilization and culture as an antidote to both the political power mongering of the

1930s and the questionable Nietzschean notion of willing into being an ever-making self. Hesse's novel, *Narcissus and Goldmund*, in many ways, highlights how the faithful Narcissus (Hesse's deeper probes into the meaning of the word) was the real builder and preserver of all that is good and beautiful in a cultural way that only the creative Goldmund understands at the end of his all too human journey---much the same theme is played out in a rawer and more graphic manner in *Demian* and *Steppenwolf*.

The Journey to the East does need to be set both within the context of Hesse's larger literary vision and the historic times in which he lived — often neither is done, hence the book is misread. And, to conclude, there is a significant if indirect political dimension at the core and centre of *The Journey to the East* that is often missed. Hopefully, this missive might correct some obvious omissions and oversights in a reading of this timely (then and now) beauty of a book.

6

THE GLASS BEAD GAME
Then and Now

What is the "Glass Bead Game"? In the idyllic poem "Hours in the Garden" (1936), which he wrote during the composition of his novel, Hesse speaks of "a game of thoughts called the Glass Bead Game" that he practiced while burning leaves in his garden. As the ashes filter down through the gate, he says, "I hear music and see men of the past and future. I see wise men and poets and scholars and artists harmoniously building the hundred-gated cathedral of the mind". These lines depict as personal experience that intellectual pastime that Hesse, in his novel, was to define as "the unio mystica of all separate members of the Universitas Litterarum" and that he bodied symbolically in the form of an elaborate game......... The Glass Bead Game is an act of mental synthesis through which the spiritual values of all ages are perceived as

simultaneously present and vitally alive.
Theodore Ziolkowski *Foreward: The Glass Bead Game, p. XI*

ermann Hesse won the Nobel Prize for Literature in 1946, and such an affirmation had much to do with his immense literary and artistic output over many a decade. Needless to say, his life spanned some of the most tragic events of the 20th century and Hesse was never shy about commenting on such realities. The publication of *The Journey to the East* in the early 1930s was, in many ways, a primer and pointer to his more developed novel, *The Glass Bead Game* (published in German in 1943). The role of Leo and the League in *The Journey to the East* anticipates, in most ways, the more sophisticated Joseph Knecht and Castalia in *The Glass Bead Game*. The nature of the game, as mentioned above by Ziolkowski, is about the threading together, in one grand synthesis and unity, the best that has been thought, said and done throughout the history of human time across civilizations, cultures, religions, literatures, philosophies, music and the arts. Obviously, such a catholic sweep of thought towards a higher unity is meant to correct and question the tendency towards disunity, fragmentation, nationalisms and all those tribalist tendencies that are so much a part of the human condition and world history.

The vision of the Castalians was, therefore, to bring together that which was separate, to unite that which was fragmented, to offer peace rather than war, to envision that which might be rather than what is. In short, Castalians were visionaries of an idealistic unity rather than a crude realism that divides one from the other. The irony of *The Glass Bead Game* is, of course, the inability of the Castalians (and Joseph Knecht-Magister Ludi) to thread together thought and action, ideal and reality, intellectual and historic events. This was the time tried warning of a sage of sorts who had seen, all too clearly, the consistent gap between those who envision a higher unity at the level of thought yet at the level of action, are continuously undermined by armies and power. At the heart and core of Hesse's probes in *The Glass Bead Game* is the tensions that exist between those, at an intellectual level, who create paradigms, models, and glass bead games of unity and those, at a historic level of life in the valley (rather than the mountain peaks of untroubled historic reality) who undermine such an intellectual game.

I mentioned above that *The Glass Bead Game* was published in German in 1943 and, in English in 1969. The tome dwells in the nexus of ideal and reality, unity and divisiveness, intellectual and historic events. The message offered cannot be missed. The translation of the longing for some higher unity of thought is often thwarted in the realm of human doing, willing and action. Even the final death of Knecht leaves the future open, but if the past was to be any teacher into the future, utopian idealism had to be seen for what it was. Who, though, are some of the contemporary Castalians and Glass Bead Players of the early decades of the 21st century and what might Hesse's epic novel yet speak to them? I will, for the remainder of this essay, ponder eight glass bead game players and their clan.

The Four Horsemen of the New Atheists

THERE has, in the last few years, emerged a group of thinkers called the four horsemen of the New Atheism: Hitchens, Dennett, Harris and Dawkins. Hitchens died a couple of years ago, and with the addition of Ayaan Hirsi Ali, the group might be called the four riders of the New Atheism. Needless to say, the intellectual game played by this group tends to pit science against religion (rather dated and superficial) to the detriment of religion and elevation of science. This approach to the historic religion-science conflict is neither good religion nor science---it is scientism and religiosity. But, the New Atheists do not see it that way. They are on a crusade in which the ideas and reality of science are threaded together in the game in such a way that science is almost seen as the saviour of the world, and religion the means of its deterioration. This either-or, black-white way of thinking, obviously so, leads to an ongoing conflict between religion and science and tends to be rather crude and simplistic. Most thoughtful theologians and sophisticated religious thinkers and activists can scarcely recognize themselves in such a notion of religion and few are the good scientists that are fully on board with the New Atheists. There is at a much higher level a fine dialogue (and has been for centuries) between religion and science, theology and legitimate scientific research. It is important to note, though, that this played game, by the New Atheists, although far from Hesse's vision of integration and unity tends to be trendy at a popular level these days, and, as such, needs to be flagged but not taken with a great deal of seriousness. Those who are truly serious about the religion-science issue should turn to more sophisticated sources (and there are many).

The New Physics, Taoism and Religion

IF the New Atheists tend to pit religion against science in their glass bead game of sorts, the New Physics is more interested in bringing together religion and science. There is an unhelpful tendency amongst some of those committed to the New Physics to pit Newtonian thought against the more modern ideas of physics. The publication in 1975 of Fritjof Capra's *The Tao of Physics* brought together, in a creative manner, spirituality and science. Capra's *The Turning Point* (1982) inspired the 1990 movie, *Mindwalk*. Capra has played a significant role in bringing together ecology, spirituality and science, and his recent book, *The Systems of Life*, embodies this unified vision — the glass bead game does ever continue. Capra, an Austrian, worked together with David Steindl-Rast (A Christian Benedictine monk) to publish *Belonging to the Universe* in 1991. The fact that Capra and Steindl-Rast have much in common on their journey has made it more than clear that religion need not be pitted against science. There are many who have heeded and heard Capra's clarion like call which is quite different than the New Atheists. There is a sense, of course, in which Capra (and peers) are very much well heeled Castalians and play the game of integration, systems and unity well and wisely. Capra has, legitimately so, tapped into Thomas Kuhn's *The Structure of Scientific Revolutions* to highlight the fact that science, like any other intellectual activity, works with interpretive models and when the interpretive model does not adequately deal with the new facts, new models must be brought to the fore. Such was the move made by Capra to articulate how physics, when read and interpreted in a certain way, need not be in opposition to religion and spirituality. There are many who nod a hearty amen to Capra and tribe in their approach and, in many ways, Hesse would be impressed by how well such a game is being played. How close, though, are such Castalians to the historic events troubling Europe and North America at the present time? We hear little from them in a substantive way other than idealistic slogans and clichés — such would be Hesse's warnings and insights.

Pierre Teilhard de Chardin and Thomas Berry: Evolution and Spirituality

THERE can be no doubt that Pierre Teilhard de Chardin has waxed in significance and import since his death in 1955. The fact that de Chardin, as an archeologist-paleontologist-theologian, attempted to overcome the sad and tragic schism between science and religion is part of his appeal and genius. De Chardin also attempted to spiritualize the evolutionary process in a way that undercut a purely materialist read of the unfolding of human and natural history. It was this synthesis of religion and science, a reading and interpreting of evolution that blended matter and spirit and his Christological telos of sorts that has made de Chardin a mentor for many in the post-de Chardin era. The fact that de Chardin was marginalized by the Roman Catholic establishment in his life (as was Galileo) adds to the appeal, for many, of de Chardin's insights and significant contributions to the science-religion- evolution dialogue. We have certainly moved a substantive distance from the confrontational approach to religion-science in the New Atheists when we encounter the more subtle, integrative and probing work of Pierre Teilhard de Chardin. There can be no doubt, though, that de Chardin is engaged in a playing of the glass bead game in which he is seeking to unify the ideas and reality of religion, spirituality, science and evolution within a grander meta-narrative or epic sweep of thought — such is the vocation of Castalians.

Many are those who have come to focus on de Chardin and ways and means to interpret him. There are many more, though, who draw from the well of de Chardin's thinking but go beyond his approach in the playing of the game of integrating ideas: such is the creative life of Thomas Berry. There is a sense in which Berry is a more interesting thinker than de Chardin for the simple reason he is integrating more into his field of thought than de Chardin did. Berry saw himself as an "ecotheologian", "geologian" and "earth scholar" who, rightly so, realized a "New Story" had to be told about how humanity was to live within the unfolding reality on earth, our island home. The fact that Berry was as interested in healing the religion-science divide as he was the larger political and economic issues makes him a compelling glass bead player---he was, in most ways, threading beads of thought together that de Chardin never did. Berry thought the "great work" before us was to integrate a fourfold realm of synthesis: political-legal, economic-industrial, education and religion. It was this fourfold work that was before humanity in the next phase and stage of the evolutionary process in our global village. The fact that Berry's work was included in the fine 2007 film, *What a Way to Go: Life at the End of Empire*, should be duly recognized. There can be no doubt that Berry is a Castalian of the highest order and he has been amply rewarded for playing the game well and wisely. Magister Ludi would have nodded a gracious amen to the work of Thomas Berry — he has certainly carried the work of de Chardin to a higher level and, as such, should be recognized and honoured for doing so. But, as Hesse rightly noted in *The Glass Bead Game*, such intellectual acts and events of unity in the world of the Castalians often bear little fruit in the actual world of the *vita activa* in the valley of historic political and economic events.

The work of de Chardin and Berry continues to ripple forth in the work, to a lesser degree, of Brian Swimme. Swimme, like de Chardin and Berry, is engaged in overcoming the chasm between religion and science, and Swimme's earlier academic life with Matthew Fox and tribe embodies such a furthering forth into such terrain. Swimme's commitment to evolutionary cosmology or the epic of evolution, in a positive and upward sweep, is generously reflected in his 2011 *Canticle to the Cosmos*. There can be no doubt that Swimme is carrying forth the vision of de Chardin and Berry in a way that, in thought, if not in realized deed, reflects the ongoing nature of the glass bead game:

integration, unification, dot connecting and concord. I would suggest, though, that of the three thinkers mentioned, Berry is by far the most creative and advanced glass bead game player.

The 2nd Axial Age: Karl Jaspers and Ewert Cousins

KARL Jaspers was, probably, one of the most creative philosophers of the 20th century. His friendship with Hannah Arendt and Martin Heidegger makes for a significant study in and of itself. But, it was Jaspers' theory of axial ages that is most pertinent for us. Jaspers suggested that from the 8th to 2nd centuries BCE there was an emergence of creative spirituality that altered the direction of world history: Buddhism, Jewish prophets, Plato-Aristotle, Indian Upanishads, Confucius-Lao Tzu and Zoroastrianism emerged on the stage of world history and offered a deeper and fuller notion of the faith journey than mere superstition and tribalism. The emergence of a sort of implicit universalism was birthed at such a period of the 1st axial age. But, such a birthing never truly matured and bore much fruit other than in different religions (that often turned on one another). It was with the tragedy of WWII that Jaspers sensed that we had entered the 2nd axial age. The evidence of both humanity slaughtering one another and the possibilities of a higher theological and philosophical unity pointing the way to a new age became evident to Jaspers. The world had shrunk with modernity, cultures and civilizations lived nearer one another and the potential existed for such religions to be committed to their deeper and more explicit unity. The age of Christendom and Christianity was past. The 2nd axial age would bring together all the major and minor religions of the world for a higher global end and purpose—such was the promise and hope of the post WWII 2nd axial age and, in some ways, the United Nations was on the forefront of such an experiment.

Jaspers' enucleation of the 2nd axial age beginning after WWII has become a developed manifesto of sorts for many in the game of religious and political synthesis since Jaspers death in 1969. One of the leading lights of such a visionary and unfolding evolutionary perspective is Ewert Cousins. Cousins was one of the front edge thinkers in the latter half of the 20th century in the area of contemplative interfaith dialogue, and his leadership in such comprehensive texts in spirituality, *Classics of Western Spirituality* and *World Spirituality: An Encyclopedic History of the Religious Quest* have positioned Cousins at the forefront of modern glass bead game players. The fact Cousins assisted in the coordinating of the "Spiritual Summit Conference" at the United Nations in 1975 and in 1998 co-created "The World Commission on Global Consciousness and Spirituality" cannot be missed. Cousins has certainly updated and threaded together (with many other Castalians), in this our 2nd axial age, a vision of ecological spirituality that brings together the best and noblest within each of the religions of the emerging world consciousness as a vanguard of sorts. The publication of Cousins *Christ of the 21st Century* in 1992 augured the way forward from which Cousins went much further in his global synthesis and interfaith meta-narrative. There are many who have both drawn from Jaspers and Cousins (since Cousins death in 2009), including John Hick and the more popular Karen Armstrong, but the point to note is that each and all are engaged in threading together on the necklace of thought the combined contemplative wisdom of world religions as we move ever forward, on the inevitable evolving human journey, to a better, more just and peaceful world. How would Hesse and Magister Ludi respond to such contemplative and wisdom seeking Castalians?

The Bahai Tradition: A Castalian Synthesis

THE 19th century witnessed the emergence of many religious groups but "The Bab" and "Baha-u-llah" embodied a form of religious synthesis that went beyond Islam and many Arab religions. Baha-u-llah let it be known by 1863 that a new vision for humanity was afoot that would transcend each of the world religions and find a new unified centre. Each of the historic religions were to be honoured yet raised to a higher unified level which was embodied in

"Baha-u-llah's" courageous life and teachings. Needless to say, there was no notion at this point of a 2nd axial age, but the underlying premises of the Bahai Tradition anticipates (as do other groups in the 19th century such as the Theosophical Society) many of the same ideas that Jaspers, Cousins and others of 2nd axial age ideology hold near and dear. It is rather pertinent and significant to ponder why many within the 2nd axial age tribe have not become Bahai or why Bahai's have not joined the 2nd axial age tribe. There are some obvious differences in whose synthesis should be accepted and why. This is always a telling and perennial dilemma for those who play the glass bead game of unity and harmony. What should be drawn from various traditions, what rejected and whose synthesis should be heeded and why? This is a common challenge for those who play the glass bead game and the stubborn fact that there are various types of Castalians who don't agree with one another on what should be unified and why, in a Hegelian like dialectic, must be faced into and not flinched from. But, the Bahai tradition certainly is a formal and institutional way of playing the game, but many from the traditions it claims to draw from strongly disagree with how their traditions are read and interpreted to fit into the unified puzzle of religious unity and concord. It is important to note, in this overview, that the Bahai tradition is but a player in the glass bead game, although many differ and disagree with its end point and penultimate synthesis. Again, whose version of unity should have the final word and why?

The Primordial Tradition: Exoteric and Esoteric Religion

THE Primordial Tradition has held the attention and interest of many for a significant amount of time. Some of the finest thinkers and activists are committed to such a perennial way. What, in short, is the essence of the Primordial Tradition and who are some of its finest apologists? The core of the Primordial Tradition can be summed briefly by this approach---there is an exoteric pathway within all the major and minor religions in which theology, myths, liturgies, philosophy, rituals and sacred texts define the tradition. The realms of the exoteric are legitimate and necessary pathways to transformation, insight, enlightenment and wisdom. Each and all on their journey should belong to a specific tradition that points to greater depths and heights. But, the exoteric route is but a lower level on the pilgrimage and quest for meaning. It is the mystics, contemplatives or sages within each tradition that, at an esoteric level, embody the essence of each tradition, and, at an essential and esoteric level, all the religions converge and are one. It is this exoteric-esoteric distinction that defines the Primordial tradition and illuminates why those committed to such a way are Castalians and glass bead players.

Who are some of the thinkers of such a heritage? Some of the most prominent are Rene Guenon, Fritjof Schuon, Martin Lings, Ananda Coomaraswamy and Seyyed Nasr to name but a few. Huston Smith is, probably, one of the best popularizers of such a tradition just as Nasr's Gifford Lectures, *Knowledge of the Sacred* (1981), in thoughtful and probing detail describes such a historic and philosophic position. William Quinn's *The Only Tradition* (1997) and Darrol Bryant's *Woven on the Loom of Time: Many Faiths and One Divine Purpose* (1999) reflect such a perspective, Bryant, in many ways, an echo of Huston Smith.

There can be no doubt that the Primordial Tradition reflects a subtle way of playing the glass bead game. It is questionable, though, whether mystics and contemplatives at the esoteric level are on the same page not only within traditions but between traditions. Again, we are faced with the question of whose version of the Ultimate has final authority, hence what will be ignored from the exoteric level on the way to the integrative esoteric level? There can be no doubt that the players from the Primordial Tradition have been trained well in their version of Castalia, but their version of concord and unity is not necessarily the same as other Castalians and glass bead players---such is the perennial tensions and clashes within the family of Castalians.

Bede Griffiths and Universal Wisdom

BEDE Griffiths was a dear friend of C.S. Lewis and Lewis dedicated his 2nd autobiography, *Surprised by Joy*, to Griffiths. Lewis and Griffiths journeyed to Christianity together, but as the life of Griffiths unfolded he became one of the most significant Roman Catholic contemplatives of the 20th century. Much attention tends to be focussed on Thomas Merton in the West, but Griffiths had an equal range of depth and breadth. The further Griffiths faith pilgrimage, the greater his interest in Indian-Hindu-Christian dialogue and, in time, his growing commitment to spirituality-science (de Chardin, Rupert Sheldrake and Thomas Berry to name a few), ecology, feminism and social justice. The many books and articles Griffiths published speak legions about the way he, like a conductor in an orchestra, brought all the musicians and instruments together to play in one great harmony — such is the glass bead game and Griffiths was, in many ways, a Magister Ludi, true to Hesse's notion of Joseph Knecht as one who serves. The edited tome by Beatrice Bruteau (yet another player of sorts), *Bede Griffiths and the Hindu-Christian Dialogue: The Other Half of my Soul*, goes well beyond Griffiths in depth commitment to Christian-Hindu dialogue--- poetry, science, memories of Griffiths as a person, 2nd axial age devotees such as Paul Knitter, Matthew Fox and, of course, Wayne

Teasdale grace the pages, each and all being integrative glass bead players. The close relationship between Griffiths and Raimon Panikkar should be noted also, both men front and centre in articulating a larger vision of concord and unity, common grace and general revelation. The final tome by Griffiths, edited by Roland Ropers, *Universal Wisdom: A Journey through the Sacred Wisdom of the World* is a must read for those keen to enter the ever-expanding range of Griffiths' life and thought. Many have been the followers of Griffiths, but Wayne Teasdale (more than most when alive) conducted yet more the grand orchestra. The New Camaldoli Monastery in Big Sur/California is a site and centre of Griffiths' admiration and support. I was fortunate in April 2018 to be a "Scholar in Residence" at the Monastery (I have been there in previous years) and lived in Bruno Barnhardt's cell. Barnhardt, Robert Hale, Thomas Matus and the present Prior, Cyprian Consiglio, are each and all, in their different ways, on much the same page as Griffiths—exquisite glass bead players and Castalians in a monastic context---Hesse would have understood the appeal and need for such a lived contemplative community in which to string together the beads of thought to make yet a finer necklace for the future.

Ken Wilber and Integration

KEN Wilber has been a guide and tutor for many in the last few decades, as a generalist of sorts, committed to integrating various ways of thinking into one grand and visionary whole. Wilber has tried to bring together spirituality, science, politics, ecology and many other aspects of the human journey that are often kept separate and discrete. Again, such an approach is a critique and counter to various forms of postmodern fragmentation and divisiveness, the large and epic interpretive narrative points the way to a future of unity. Needless to say, we have travelled a long journey from the New Atheists by the time we have heeded and heard Wilber (and others I have mentioned in the last few sections). Wilber, as founder of the Integral Institute is, as the name suggests, about integration and his latest book, *The Religion of Tomorrow: A Vision for the Future of the Great Traditions*, engages in his notion of integration. As mentioned above, many are those inclined towards unity, integration and concord, but the tension emerges when each and all differ on how such an integration is to occur and why. The situation is much the same within the Great Traditions who hold high a sacred text as their authority yet differ on how the text is to be interpreted and why.

Each group within a Tradition thinks their read is the best and others differ with them, hence divisions within a Tradition. The same is the case with those who play the glass bead game—whose version should be heeded and why? Wilber is one version of integration but there are others. It is significant in *The Glass Bead Game* that when Joseph Knecht visited Father Jacobus at Mariafels Monastery these very issues were front and centre for them. But, deeper still, there is an appeal, charm and allure to the history of intellectual events and an orchestral concert of thought by those who participate in the game. But, what is the relationship between being cloistered away at an aesthetic and uplifting event for soul and mind, imagination and harmony that, when concert is done, the busy world of the *vita activa* of historic events has not really changed? What, in short, is the relationship between the level of visionary thought about unity, concord, harmony, integration and oneness and the real world of historic events where human nature and public life collide and counter such idealistic and utopian notions? Such was the final note of warning by Hesse in *The Glass Bead Game*. If idealists do not factor into their reflections the complex, contradictory, layered and duplicitous tendencies of human nature, then the finest ideas will never substantively root and bear fruit. This was Hesse's warning — don't be naïve about the possibilities of intellectual activities bringing together a better world — there are those who have power and will another agenda. Hesse lived through WWI and WWII and he knew of what he spoke. *The Glass Bead Game* is a perennial reminder of tensions between idealism and realism, unity and divisiveness, thought and will or, to use St. Augustine's distinction (Hesse died in his sleep with a copy of Augustine's *Confessions* on his chest), *caritas* and *cupiditas*.

The Glass Bead Game raises questions at two levels and such questions will ever be with us: 1) whose version of unity, integration, concord, harmony and oneness should be heeded and why and 2) what is the relationship between those who play the contemplative and wisdom glass bead game of unity and the reality of actual political events in the world which seem to simply ignore the players of the game who often dwell in a naïve and cloistered intellectual enclave? The fact Magister Ludi died as he made the transition from Castalia (drowning in the lake as he was about to instruct the young Tito) can be read in different ways. Was a death needed by both Castalians (contemplative intellectuals) and activists to, phoenix like, bring in a new way of reconfiguring the *vita contemplativa-vita activa* or were the Titos of the future forever fated to live within such an unresolved and unresolvable tension and dilemma? Such are the questions Hesse left us with in, probably, one of the finest novels of the 20th century and all time---a must read for those grappling with the substantive issues of thought and action on our all too human journey.

7

HESSE AND MERTON
Affinities

"But the longing to get on the other side of everything already settled, this makes me, and everybody like me, a road sign to the future."
Hermann Hesse *Wandering: Farmhouse*

"There is another side of Kanchenjunga and of every mountain---the side that has never been photographed and turned into postcards. That is the only side worth seeing."
Thomas Merton, November 19 1968

It is rather surprising, given the fact that Hermann Hesse and Thomas Merton are two of the pre-eminent countercultural ikons of the latter half of the 20th century, that few are the articles, books or essays that have brought them together and pondered their obvious affinities. John Collins has, in a suggestive way, pointed to affinities between Hesse and Merton by reflecting on Merton's readings of Hesse's *Journey to the East, Steppenwolf* and *Siddhartha*, but beyond Collins' two articles, there is nothing of substance and significance that examines the countercultural affinities between Hesse and Merton (and there are many). Hopefully, this missive will correct such a lack and omission.

Hesse was a generation older than Merton, being born in 1877, Merton being born in 1915, but both men were acutely sensitive to the pressing issues of western culture and many of the dominant dangers that threatened to undermine and negate the deeper longings that make for a more meaningful life journey. I have, since the 1970s, read most of Merton's books and written a few books and articles on Merton, and Hesse has been a fellow pilgrim of sorts for many a decade. I have spent some lovely time at Hesse's home on the upper rock knoll in Montagnola in Switzerland, imbibing the landscape, air, site and scenery that so held Hesse and from which most of his writings were birthed. So, in some ways, Hesse and Merton have been mentors for me on my journey. This essay is my way of repaying them for all they have taught me and passed my way.

Theodore Ziolkowski (a fine Hesse scholar) penned *Saint Hesse among the Hippies* (American German Review: v. 35, no. 2, 1969) many a decade ago and the 1990 graduating essay by James Black, *Hesse and the Hippies: The Sociology of a Literary Phenomenon* tells its own convincing tale. Ziolkowski and Black make it abundantly clear that Hesse was one of the primary portals for many counterculture types in the 1960s-1970s into a vision of faith and life that could not be co-opted by a scientistic, secular or technological notion of the human journey or the literary Sanhedrin of the time. There were many writers and activists that shaped, formed and inspired the counterculture, but Hesse's multiple writings (poems, prose, novels, paintings etc.) acted as a rite of passage for many into the counterculture. Many of the hippies of the 1960s-1970s seriously misread Hesse and reduced him to a shallow plaything of their notion of a counterculture (which led, in some ways, to his virtual disappearance the last few decades), but, at a deeper and more substantive level, for those who read Hesse aright, he was a counterculture alternate to the establishment ethos of the 1960s-1970s (even though he died in 1962). Hesse had anticipated, though, through his soul searching and layered political commentaries such as those found in *If the War Goes On* (1948) a close relationship between the contemplative and the political.

William Shannon, in his compact and succinct book, *Something of a Rebel: Thomas Merton: His Life and Works: An Introduction* (1997), rightly suggests Merton has been read in two ways: "one, ascetic, conservative, traditional and monastic; the other, radical, independent and somewhat akin to beats and hippies and poets (p. 127). It is the Merton that is "akin to beats and hippies and poets" who has much affinity with Hesse among the hippies. Many of Merton's writings in the 1960s did have many an affinity with the counterculture. I have dealt with this in my recently edited, *Thomas Merton and the Counterculture: A Golden String* (2016) and my earlier *Thomas Merton and the Beats of the North Cascades* (2006). There can be no doubt, therefore, that both Hesse and Merton were on frontstage within the Christian and Interfaith counterculture of the 1960s-1970s. What were, though, their affinities that have often been ignored in writings about Hesse and Merton?

There are five areas I will lightly but not substantively land on when dealing with the affinities between Hesse and Merton: 1) pioneers of the 20th century contemplative renaissance, 2) west meets east, 3) contemplation and the arts, 4) contemplation and correspondence and 5) contemplation and prophetic vision. Each of these areas placed Hesse and Merton in a countercultural position in regards to the prevailing and dominant cultural ethos of their time and era.

Pioneers of 20th Century Contemplative Renaissance

THE West has been significantly dominated since the 16th century by a reversal of the *vita contemplativa* by the *vita activa*. The Western classical tradition once held high the *vita contemplativa* as a way of knowing and being from which the *vita activa* emerged in a wise and just manner. The rise of the protestant work ethic (and its secularization) has meant the *vita activa* has come to define and shape identity, the soul and society in the west. Even though the language of liberty is viewed as the great good, most are merely victims of their drivenness, hence not truly free. Hesse and Merton realized, all too clearly, how and why the contemplative way had been marginalized and banished and the consequences of such a cultural and spiritual reality. Both also realized that for a civilization to be truly free, fit and healthy, the contemplative way had to be retrieved and recalled. This would mean, though, digging deep into the divided and conflicted souls of those who had too substantively imbibed and internalized the *vita activa*.

Hesse was, of course, much more the novelist than Merton, and in most of his novels he examines and explores the complex nature of the human soul, desires gone askew, temperaments off balance and the longing for recovery, unity and inner equilibrium. Novels such as *Demian, Narcissus and Goldmund* and

Steppenwolf illuminate, in graphic depth and detail, the tensions and clashes that emerge when the inner quest is not properly ordered. The resolution to such novels does emerge, though, in an initial way, in *Siddharta* and a more mature manner in *Journey to the East* and *The Glass Bead Game* (Hesse's final and most mature novel). It is significant in such novels that Hesse holds high and clarifies the meaning of the contemplative, *The Glass Bead Game* being Hesse's summa on the issue and one of the reasons Hesse won the Nobel Prize for Literature in 1946.

It would be impossible to read Merton without becoming aware of his passion to dive and delve ever deeper into the contemplative journey. The Epilogue in *The Seven Story Mountain* touches on "Active and Contemplative Orders", one of Merton's early books was *Seeds of Contemplation* (the more mature version being *New Seeds of Contemplation)* and most of Merton's writings, in the 1950s, in one genre or another, dealt with the contemplative journey. In fact, I think it could be argued that Merton was, probably, one of the most significant miners of the mother lode of the contemplative in the latter half of the 20th century. Merton saw all so clearly that the West had become addicted to the *vita activa* and such an addiction had become an oppressive bondage. The contemplative path was the means to liberate an imprisoned culture from such an addiction. It is significant that of the eight themes that Shannon sees as defining Merton's journey, the contemplative (2: "Prayer: The Journey Toward Interiority: Contemplative Spirituality) is a core one.

There can be little doubt that Hesse and Merton, like the perennial canaries in the mine shaft, felt the toxins of the modern *vita activa* and, in their different ways, they questioned such an imperial way of knowing and being. Hesse was not a monk like Merton, but his life at Montagnola in southern Switzerland certainly embodied a contemplative dimension. Merton was a monk, but one of his perpetual frustrations was the way the monastic life which was, in principle, meant to be contemplative, had become excessively busy and active.

West Meets East

THERE has been an unhealthy but understandable tendency by many raised in the West to assume the West is about science, industry, secularism and a hyper activism that is lacking in wisdom and the contemplative. This has meant many of the more astute and sensitive westerners have pitted the knowledge driven activist West against the more wisdom oriented and contemplative East. Such a simplistic dualism, of course, distorts both the Occident and Orient, but this has been a tendency amongst some of the more naïve. The West and East, in such a scenario, are either seen as complementary or, worse case, the West is demonized and the East idealized (or the reverse can occur, also). How did Hesse and Merton approach the Western and Eastern civilizational realities?

Hesse grew up in a prominent German pietistic family (Swabian Pietism) with many a connection via missionary and educational work to India. He came in time to question substantive aspects of his Swabian pietism, but he also had a deep respect for such a heritage. This is clearly spelled out in "The Fourth Life" which did not make it into *The Glass Bead Game*. The first and longer version of "The Fourth Life" walks the reader into the nuanced pathway of Hesse's early years. Hesse realized, only too clearly, that his German pietistic upbringing tended to distort the sheer breadth and depth of Christianity, hence his ongoing attraction to the contemplative depths of the Roman Catholic tradition we see played out in *The Glass Bead Game*, Father Jacobus and the Benedictines being tutors and teachers to Joseph Knecht (Magister Ludi).

"Father Confessor" in *The Glass Bead Game* walks the attentive reader into the wisdom and contemplative dimensions of patristic and desert spirituality that so attracted Merton (*The Wisdom of the Desert*). "The Father Confessor" life, in some ways, anticipates Merton's *The Wisdom of the Desert*. There is much more that could be said about Hesse's critical yet appreciative understanding of both Roman Catholic and German pietistic Lutheranism.

Hesse judiciously weighed, again and again, the riches offered by the West, but he also realized the East had much to offer that had been lost by the West. I mentioned above that *Siddhartha* was one of Hesse's early forays into the East (it was translated into English in 1951 and published by New Directions who Merton often published with), and this missive has held many — Siddhartha is not the enlightened Buddha but rather a man in search of meaning in a world that often demeans, distorts or offers multiple distractions and diversions from meaning — obviously, Indian thought, Hinduism and Buddhism loom large and factor significant in this primer of the 1920s. But, Hesse's deeper probes into the Orient and the Orient-Occident are in *The Journey to the East* and *The Glass Bead Game*.

The fact that Hesse drew judiciously and discerningly from the Western Christian Tradition (ignored by many) must also be balanced by the fact he had a keen and abiding interest in the contributions from the Eastern heritage. Hesse's earliest book, *Peter Camenzind* (1904) is a running commentary of sorts on east-west spirituality and the wisdom offered by the best of both traditions just as his earlier short story, *Friends* (1907-1908), highlights the literary fact that genuine friends will be guided in their quest for deeper contemplative insight by mining both the wisdom of the west and east. Much of Hesse's mid and later life writings return again and again to the need to draw from the best of the wisdom traditions of the world while also critically reflecting on their questionable elements. As mentioned above, *The Journey to the East* and *The Glass Bead Game* bring together some of Hesse's finest thinking on the west-east dialogue.

The fact Thomas Merton was drawn to the Roman Catholic Church as the Tridentine paradigm was waning meant that he both accepted such a model but doubted its staying power. *The Seven Storey Mountain* (even though selling well but not reflecting Merton at its mature best) lacked any substantive sense of Merton engaging the East-West issue. The guru the young Merton met, Brahmachari, did suggest Merton delve into his own tradition before he wandered afield into the Orient.

Most of Merton's journey in the 1940s-1950s embodied and reflected the advice of the Hindu sage. But, by the late 1950s-1960s, Merton was very much on the same page as Hesse was decades earlier. Zen Buddhism was in vogue at the time, and Merton's dialogues with D.T. Suzuki are well known and noted. Merton explored others aspects of Buddhism with the Dalai Lama, Thich Nhat Hanh and other Buddhist monks as is well recorded in *The Asian Journal* (in which he wrote a Preface to the Indian classic *The Bhagavad Gita*). Merton also was keen on understanding Judaism in its mystical forms and his friendship with Abraham Heschel is foundational in this area. Islamic Sufism and Hinduism (Merton's primer on Gandhi is a must read) also drew Merton as did 1st Nations spirituality as reflected in *Ishi Means Man*. The Chinese Taoist heritage also had a substantive impact on Merton's journey as reflected in *Mystics and Zen Masters* and *The Way of Chuang Tzu*. The primer, with an introduction by the Canadian, George Woodcock, *Thomas Merton: Thoughts on the East* (New Directions book: 1995) is a portal into Merton's commitment to understanding the Occident on its terms while being deeply grounded in the contemplative vision of Christianity, also.

There can be no doubt that Merton, like Hesse, in their commitment to the contemplative way, turned to the Orient and Occident for guidance and wisdom. Both men thoughtfully weighed the pro-contra of such civilizational ways of interpreting the contemplative journey. There was none of the idealizing of the East, denigrating of the West in their more mature reflections. Hesse, like Merton, attempted to draw together the best of both traditions in their thinking and life. I don't think they can be reduced to syncretists or pluralists though. There is much more to them then such trendy interpretive approaches. I think both men, for different reasons, can be seen as committed Christians with a high view (higher than most) of common grace or natural theology. This deeper catholic notion has often led to their being misunderstood by those with a more dogmatic and rational approach to the contemplative way and interfaith dialogue

Contemplation and the Arts

THERE has been, sadly so, a narrow way of viewing philosophy in the last few centuries. A certain form of empiricism and science has come to dominate and philosophical positivism has genuflected to such a methodology. Reason is then seen as a faculty or organ that brings to the clearing objective knowledge via inductive, deductive or sense driven empirical research. This has meant that philosophy as the longing or love of wisdom has been reduced to defining terms, language games and logic. This approach to philosophy has tended to undermine and undercut the classical and historic understanding of philosophy as a contemplative journey into insight, wisdom and transformation.

The historic fact that philosophy has been, to some degree, co-opted by positivism has meant that those committed to the deeper and older meaning of philosophy have often turned to the arts as a means of knowing and being. Hesse and Merton were certainly no uncritical fans of philosophy as positivism and both men expressed their contemplative journey much more through artistic means than a narrow philosophic process. This is one of the reasons their appeal has been so far reaching in the 20th century (and beyond).

Jacob Burckhardt was, in the latter half of the 19th century, a creative cultural historian who articulated, in a way few were doing at the time, alternate ways to interpret the Italian Renaissance and Classical Greek thought. Burckhardt lived most of his most fruitful years in Basel, and Hesse, as a young and feeling his way artist, spent time in Basel. It was impossible to live in Basel and not come under the spell of Burckhardt. Jacob Burkhardt, for different reasons, had an unusual impact on both the life and writings of Nietzsche and Hesse. Burkhardt, for good or ill, tended to be suspicious (and there were reasons to be so) of those who took an uncritical attitude towards the state and church (and their uneasy union). Burkhardt held culture, at its purest and best, as a countervailing and necessary antidote to the failings and pretensions of state and church, politics and religion. There is a sense that Nietzsche (of whom Hesse admired at times and wrote an article on) and Hesse were indebted to Burkhardt's high view of culture as higher and more substantive than religion and politics, although Hesse, unlike Nietzsche, did recognize that there are worrisome tendencies when the more aesthetic aspects of culture become ends in themselves. Hesse certainly held a higher commitment to the faith journey than did Burkhardt and Nietzsche, and he lived the trying tension between religion and culture but shared the suspicion of Burkhardt and Nietzsche about politics and a too high a view of state authority. Needless to say, Hesse saw the outworking of such an uncritical notion of the state in German throughout much of the first half of the 20th century.

The young Hesse, as I mentioned above, was born into a much-respected German pietistic family that had many a connection with India. Hesse turned away from such a way of understanding the faith journey in his late teens and very much immersed himself in the broader German and European cultural ethos (much to the chagrin of some of his family). Literature, music and the arts won and drew the maturing Hesse and his earliest publications, *Romantic Songs* (1896), *One Hour After Midnight* (1898) and *Posthumous Writings and Poems of Herman Lauscher* (1901) although not selling well (the latter better than the former two books of poetry and prose) did reflect an obvious turn to the romantic way of seeing and literary culture (a sort of surreal and dreamlike aestheticism) as a rebuke of sorts to an unfeeling and crass world of politics, religion and the captains of industry.

The further Hesse journeyed in his pilgrimage through time the more poetry and prose are balanced by the classical works of music (which work themselves, again and again, into Hesse's writings) and painting. In fact, painting comes to play a substantive role in Hesse's life, and there is definite contemplative quality in his thousands of paintings. Unfortunately, most commentators on Hesse have tended to focus on his writings, but such an approach misses the central role that art played in Hesse's life from WWI afterwards.

There can be no doubt, though, that for Hesse, music, literature and painting were the means and pathway that revealed to him the deeper realities of life and the means to express his contemplative vision. It is significant that in *The Glass Bead Game* music is the genre by which harmony and unity is brought forth from fragmentation and discrete academic disciplines amongst the Castalians.

Thomas Merton was certainly not drawn to positivism as a way of doing philosophy. Like Hesse, literature was his way of doing philosophy and the broader artistic ethos drew him. Merton had, as a mentor and model of sorts, his father and mother (who were both artists). Owen and Ruth Merton stood very much within the French impressionistic school and both studied with the much-respected Canadian artist, Percyval Tudor-Hart. The relationship between Tudor-Hart and Owen Merton was so close that in the biography of Tudor-Hart by Alasdair Alpin MacGregor, *Percyval Tudor-Hart: 1873-1954: Portrait of an Artist* (1961) a full chapter (IV) is dedicated to Owen Merton ("Tudor-Hart's Interest in Owen Merton: 1887-1931). Thomas Merton, unlike Hesse, grew up in an artistic and bohemian context before the untimely deaths of his mother, then father. Owen Merton was very much a servant of the artistic muses and culture and Thomas Merton imbibed such a way of being.

Merton was a poet, like Hesse, and although he was certainly not the gifted novelist that Hesse was (Merton's novels, *The Straights of Dover*, *Labyrinth* and *My Arguments with the Gestapo* were not the highest quality) both men were fine and probing poets. Most of Merton's earliest published books of poetry when in the monastery, *Thirty Poems* (1944), *Man in the Divided Sea* (1946), *Figures for an Apocalypse* (1948) and *Tears of the Blind Lions (1949)* are, in many ways, much more informative and insightful pathways into Merton's spiritual and literary journey than are his initial autobiography (*The Seven Storey Mountain*), biography-hagiography of Mother M. Berchmans (which he thought one of his worst books alongside *What are these Wounds?*) and his first stab at a book length prose discussion of the contemplative life (*Seeds of Contemplation*). But, it is in the appendix of sorts in *Figures for an Apocalypse* that we get a sense of Merton's thoughts on the relationship between poetry and contemplation. "Poetry and the Contemplative Life: An Essay" makes the needful yet obvious case that the arts and poetry, to be specific, are a finer and fitter way to live into and from a contemplative vision than a narrow way of doing philosophy that reduces the mind to logic and language chess games of the calculating mind.

There was much more to Merton, though, in his artistic journey than a literary rather than a pinched and constrictive way of understanding the relationship between thought, imagination and experience. Merton took to Zen sketches, photography, pop, jazz, folk music and various types of icons as means of living into the contemplative pathway. Merton was, more than Hesse, as a monk, grounded and rooted in a more disciplined monastic and religious life, but both were keenly alert to the role of culture and the arts as a suggestive way to the contemplative core and centre of our all too human journey. Hesse was not a Cistercian monk, but the contemplative monastic way factors large in his many novels, novellas and short stories. There was, in short, something deeply catholic about Hesse and this obstinate fact brings him close to Merton both in the areas of culture and religious life.

It is important to note that for Hesse and Merton, both being romantics of a higher level, that Culture and Nature had much in common. It is virtually impossible to read Hesse's writings from beginning to end without sensing and seeing his sensitive attitude towards Nature. Hesse was acutely aware that Nature had much to teach and as development accelerated and cities became more dehumanizing, Nature, when understood aright, had much to teach the soul and society---such is the romantic way. Merton, in this sense, was no different than Hesse. Both men were ecological pioneers. Monasteries, by their nature, are experiments in sustainable living and most monasteries are located far from cities. Monica Weis, more than most, has astutely seen how Merton and the monastic life embody a view of ecological consciousness. *Thomas Merton's Gethsemani: Landscapes of Paradise* (2005) is a visual and textual delight of a read that places Merton's understanding of the monastic way within a historic environmental vision. The emergence by Merton, in the 1960s, in a more conscious way, via John Muir, Aldo Leopold, Rachel Carson and aboriginal spirituality speaks much about the way he threaded together the monastic vision of the new world with many of the pressing challenges of the growing ecological concerns of the planet. Hesse and Merton, therefore, had a unique way, as high romantics, of threading together Culture and Nature in their writings and life in a way that can still inspire and challenge those alert to the pertinent issues of our ethos and age.

Contemplation and Correspondence

HESSE and Merton, for different reasons, through their confessional style of writing, won the hearts and minds of many in the 20th century. The sheer honesty and vulnerability in their poetry, novels and life drew many to both men. Readers could not help but sense in the journey of Hesse and Merton a rare gift and ability to speak to each person on their pilgrimage through time. The fact that both men needed solitude and silence to go deeper into places of insight and revelation was often missed by those who crudely and boorishly, often without invitation, arrived at their homes and hermitages expecting a generous welcome. Many were the moments when Hesse and Merton responded with legitimate frustration when religious tourists of sorts trespassed on the silence of their sacred seasons of contemplative silence. This did not mean, though, Hesse and Merton did not have a sense of responsibility to respond to those who contacted them.

The deeper the dives of Hesse and Merton, the more they recognized and realized their unity with others and the vast chasm between human longing and the lived reality of fragmentation and alienation. Many were the letters that arrived at Gethsemani and Hesse's home in Montagnola, advice being sought from sages that offered life giving advice for the soul and society. And, extremely generous were the gracious letters in reply to the questions that emerged from meaningful places. The volumes of letters now collected in multiple tomes speaks much about the way Hesse and Merton linked together their contemplative journeys and the implication of such pilgrimages in responding to the needs and questions of others.

The publication of *Soul of the Age: Selected Letters of Hermann Hesse: 1891-1962* (1991) made it more than obvious that a significant element of Hesse's literary life was correspondence. It has been estimated that there are more than 30,000 letters in the Hesse archives and Hesse kept more than 40,000 letters that had been sent his way. Some have suggested that almost 1/3 of Hesse's working hours were devoted to responding in letters. There were, of course, Hesse's letters with the literati of his time such as Thomas Mann (*The Hesse – Mann Letters*: 2005), but for a fuller read of Hesse's vast correspondence, *Hermann Hesse: Writer, Guru, Searcher* by Gabriele Ochsenbein (2012) fills in many a detail. Those who linger too long only on Hesse the writer, painter and musician miss, at an equally important level, Hesse the correspondent. It is Hesse the correspondent that speaks much about the man behind the artistic productions. At one level, Hesse was seen by many as reclusive and yet, at a more significant level, his many letters make it clear he was most giving of his time and energy.

There are those who have compared Merton's *Seven Storey Mountain* with John Henry Newman's *Apologia Pro Vita Sua*. Newman once said, "The true life of a man is in his letters". This is certainly the case with Hesse and Merton. William Shannon has suggested that "letters are a way of building and sustaining friendships. In the Merton letters you get to meet his many friends throughout the world. Letters give an insight into a person's humanness and concerns in ways that may not appear in books written for a general public. And, above all, Thomas Merton was a superb letter writer" (*Something of a Rebel*, p. 169).

There are five packed volumes of letters written by Merton to a diverse audience: 1) *The*

Hidden Ground of Love: Letters on Religious Experience and Social Concerns, 2) *The Road to Joy: Letters to New and Old Friends,* 3) *The School of Charity: Letters on Religious Renewal and Spiritual Direction,* 4) *The Courage for Truth: Letters to Writers* and 5) *Witness to Freedom: Letters in Times of Crises.* Each of these superb volumes of letters speaks much about a Merton who took careful time and attention to address a wide range of timely and timeless topics. The sheer literary output in the letters walks the reader into the life and soul of a man who took his vocation with much seriousness yet knew how to laugh at himself when ideas and issues were taken with too much seriousness.

There can be no doubt, though, that Hesse and Merton realized the essential role that correspondence played in their engagement with the world and such an art form, sadly so, has been somewhat lost in our era. Hesse and Merton have still much to teach us about some of the basics of the human journey and the role of correspondence in such a way of being.

Contemplation and Prophetic Vision

THERE has been an unhealthy and unhelpful tendency by many who turn to the meditative, contemplative and mystical way to ignore or distance themselves from the threatening and oft complex demands of such issues as war and peace, crime and punishment, poverty and wealth, ecology and economics, and technology and techne as a way of knowing and being. Such an either-or approach tends to distort the nature of a mature vision of life and is more gnostic than unitive and integrative, holistic and holy. Merton, initially, slipped into such a way of thinking in his early monastic phase, but he grew out of it by the mid-late 1950s and 1960s. The fact that Hesse lived in Europe throughout some of the most turbulent decades of the 20th century meant that he had to think seriously and substantively about the relationship between thought and action, contemplation and politics, literature and life and the trying tension of ultimate, penultimate and antepenultimate issues.

Hesse began *A Pictorial Biography* this way: "I was born toward the end of the modern times, shortly before the return of the Middle Ages, with the sign of the Archer on the ascendant and Jupiter in favourable aspect". Merton began *The Seven Storey Mountain* in a similar way: "On the last day of January 1915, under the sign of the Water Bearer, in a year of great war, and down in the shadow of some French mountains on the borders of Spain, I came into the World". Hesse certainly witnessed, in his life what the Archer and Jupiter could and did do. Merton was born when the Archer and Jupiter dominated. Both men could not retreat from the stubborn reality of war (much closer to Hesse than Merton) and the clash between war and peace was ever before them — they could not indulge in a cloistered virtue that never sallied forth.

It is significant to note that Hesse, when younger, co-edited the liberal weekly, *Marz*, which was founded in 1907 to critique the aggressive tendencies of Kaiser Wilhelm II. It was also at this period of time Hesse met Theodore Heuss (1884-1963) who was front and centre in literary and political life in Germany. Heuss became President of the Federal Republic of Germany from 1949-1959. Heuss was a warm supporter of Hesse throughout the turbulent years of Hesse's political opposition to German political life. Conrad Haussmann (1857-1922), a regular contributor to *Marz*, and a member of the Reichstag, was friends with Hesse from 1908 until his death in 1922.

Hesse's friendship with political leaders such as Heuss and Haussmann and his involvement with a variety of literary and political journals and publications meant that Hesse was keenly alert and alive to the issues of his time and how he might respond to them. The publication of many of Hesse's political writings in *If the War goes on…..* covers, in thoughtful essay form, almost 30 articles from 1914-1948 that deal with the hawkish nature of the German political ethos and more peaceful ways Germany might have gone. The essays include such classics as "Zarathustra's Return", "War and Peace", "Thou Shalt Not Kill", "A Letter to Germany", "Message to the Nobel Prize Banquet" and "On Romain Rolland" (who Hesse had a decades long friendship with).

*If the War goes on…..*covers more than 30 years of prose writing by Hesse that returns, again and again, to the war-peace dilemma that so dogged Europe in the 20th century. It cannot be denied that Hesse had a tendency to examine the deeper nature of the inner life at a spiritual and psychological level in a way that few did, but this did not deflect him from addressing the larger political issues of the time in a poignant and prophetic manner. The fact he was given the Nobel Prize for Literature in 1946 speaks much about the quality of his life and writings and their impact on European literary, cultural and political life.

Merton, as mentioned above, came into the world "in a year of great war" and war shadowed him much of his life. Merton entered the monastery about the same time that Pearl Harbour was bombed and, like Hesse, he understood the impact of war, his brother being a victim of it. Merton had to make a difficult decision, when younger, about whether he would become a Cistercian or join Catherine de Hueck Doherty in inner city New York. There is a direct line and lineage between Doherty and Dorothy Day (who Merton supported in the *Catholic Worker*) as recounted in *Comrades Stumbling Along: The Friendship of Catherine de Heuck Doherty and Dorothy Day as Revealed through Their Letters* (2009). Merton did, when entering the monastery, for a few short years in the 1940s-1950s, retreat from the larger public and political fray, but such a decision was but a season in his journey. It is impossible to miss even in *Conjectures of a Guilty Bystander* (material taken from Merton's notebooks from 1956-1966) that Merton was aware of the larger world issues beyond the enclosed walls of the monastery. Needless to say, he was often opposed when he dared to raise the larger and troubling issues in his time such as civil rights, nuclear war, Vietnam, war and peace, ecological concerns, aboriginal rights and reform within the church. Merton, like Hesse, faced much opposition and many a friend parted paths with both men the further they went down more dovish paths. I have covered Merton's peacemaking journey in my article, "Peacemaker", in *Thomas Merton: Monk on the Edge* (2012). There is a historic consistency in Hesse's writings on the larger issues of war and peace that is lacking in Merton, but there is a short season intensity on the issues by Merton lacking in Hesse. But, there can be no doubt that both men took seriously the need to integrate the spiritual and psychological dimensions of the journey with the larger political and public aspects of life. And, both men, in the way they approached the inner and outer realities (and sought to integrate them) were decidedly countercultural. I don't think any reader of the life and writings of Hesse and Merton would equate them with the dominant establishment of the time—they were, in their different ways, prophetic canaries.

Hesse and Merton: Countercultural Affinities

THERE are some historic connections between Hesse and Merton that have not been noticed. Hesse went to school for a time at the former Cistercian monastery in Maulbronn. Hesse was often drawn, in his writings, to the monastic and contemplative way. It was Henry Miller in the 1950s (when living in Big Sur) that encouraged the translation and publication by New Directions of Hesse's *Siddhartha*. This was the book Merton read and found most valuable in the final leg of his journey in Asia. There is a fine correspondence between Miller and Merton (initiated by Miller) which I tracked and discuss in "Thomas Merton and Henry Miller: Our Faces" in *Thomas Merton and the Counterculture: A Golden String* (2016). The Hesse-Miller-Merton connection is worth the probing. Hesse was just emerging as a significant North American writer in the late 1950s-1960s as Merton was nearing the end of his journey. Hesse became a guru and ikon of sorts for many in North America in the counterculture of the 1960s-1970s. Merton, by the 1960s, like William Everson, was front and centre in the Roman Catholic counterculture and making inroads into the larger North American counterculture. Hesse was more decidedly European in his life and writings, but Merton spanned the Euro-American ethos in a way Hesse never did. The fact that Hesse died in 1962 (and was waning before that) meant that he never addressed many of the pressing issues of the 1960s in the way Merton could and did. Hesse died August 9 1962 with a copy of Augustine's *Confessions* on his chest. Merton died December 10 1968 after giving a controversial lecture on Marxism and Monasticism.

There can be no doubt that Hesse and Merton were significant prophetic canaries and embodied a countercultural vision. The way both turned to the contemplative as a corrective to an over indulgent *vita activa*, their subtle dialogue between West and East, their vision of the relationship between contemplation and arts and culture, their notion of Culture and Nature as companions, their generous and gracious commitment to letter writing, correspondence, friendship and last, but not insignificant, their sense of their role and responsibility to the larger public and political issues of their age and ethos must be noted. In each and all of these, Hesse and Merton had countercultural affinities. Hopefully, in time, others will recognize this obvious reality and much more will be written on the affinities between Hesse and Merton.

8

ERASMUS, NIETZSCHE, HEIDEGGER, AND HESSE
Western Civilization
Competing Visions

There are moments in history when much hinges on decisions made by leaders and visionaries (and those who dutifully follow them). Inevitably, we all live with the consequences, for good or ill, of those who have preceded us. The early decades of the 16th century was a crossroads period in Western history in which decisions were made that have shaped and defined the West. The clash that took place in the early decades of the 16th century had much to do with the Roman Catholic Church and the rise of Protestant Christianity: Erasmus and Luther, in many ways, stand at the crossroads of such a clash. Western history is merely a playing out of their decisions at, initially, a theological and ecclesial level, then at economic, political and military levels.

What is the essence of the confrontation between Luther and Erasmus and why is western history a child of Luther rather than Erasmus? And, can such a position be reversed? These were some of the questions I pondered as my wife and I headed to Germany-Switzerland in June 2012. Luther took the position that the Roman Catholic Church could not be substantively reformed, hence he would use his liberty as a Christian man to break from the Roman Catholic tradition and initiate a new form of Christianity. Most Protestants have the DNA and genetic code of Luther in them. The argument is simple and has serious consequences. The multiple Protestant fragments and denominations are merely the predictable outcome of individuals using their liberty to create their own version of some sort of pure, remnant or true Christianity.

The problem is this; most Protestants can never agree on just what the genuine church should be like, hence the splintering in all directions. Luther took the rabbit out of the hat, and since Luther the rabbits have proliferated into many clans, warren clusters and families-- such is the protesting protestant way. The path taken at the crossroads by protestants merely splits off and off into narrower and narrower paths, each claiming their version of the way is the truest and best one.

Erasmus, like Luther, took the position that the Roman Catholic Church had to be reformed (Erasmus went deeper and further than Luther in his commitment to reform), but Erasmus also held to the position that the church was meant to be one, unity and protest was the tension Erasmus lived with. There are those that protest against the gap between ideals and reality but are not loyal too much, and there are those that are loyal but often fail to critique the institutions they are loyal to------Erasmus was loyal and committed to the unity of the church but, prophetic like, rigorously critical of the aberrations and failings of the Roman Catholic Church. Both Protestants and Roman Catholics were offended by Erasmus for different reasons. Erasmus was put on the Index in the 16th century, and was not removed until the 20th century at Vatican II. Luther and followers could never quite forgive Erasmus for not leaving the Roman Catholic Church. Erasmus would have seen such a move as short sighted and letting the genii of fragmentation out of the bottle. Most of western culture today (religious or secular) is merely acting out the script Luther prepared for them---rights of the individual to choose in good conscience their own way inevitably leads to the loss of a centre and multiple fragments and divisions.

Our journey to Europe took us, initially, to Basel and Freiburg where Erasmus spent the last

15 years of his life. Protestants took over Basel in 1529, and Erasmus fled to Freiburg where he lived, for the most part, from 1529-1535. I spent a significant amount of time at the Cathedral in Basel where Erasmus is buried pondering the two different paths taken by Luther and Erasmus and the consequences on western history of such decisions: protest and fragmentation or protest within a commitment to unity?---the consequences are momentous. Many westerners are either religious or secular protestants---protest and splintering dominates the day---it's all very liberal and culturally trendy. It is the Erasmian tradition that is more counter-cultural. There are few who have internalized the Erasmian approach to the inner life, church life and public life.   My European pilgrimage began, consciously so, at the beginning of the multiple splintering and fragmentation in the West. Can such a protestant tradition be reversed? Such was my meditation as I sat at the graveside in the Cathedral in Basel where Erasmus lies at rest, still waiting for those to hear what he has yet to say. I did my best to turn my ear and soul to what still needed to be heard---a divided church is certainly a weaker church than a united one, and a united church is what those of faith are meant to embody in thought, word and deed rather than the denominational tribalism we live with these days. It did not take much time (ideas have consequences) for the protesting spirit to go in a variety of directions. Why not protest

against protestant Christianity? This was the direction of certain forms of science, but there were also those who took the positions that protestant Christianity and Tridentine Catholicism had lost and forfeited a greater spiritual and intellectual depth. The search was on by the honest seekers for what was lost in the clash between Protestants and Roman Catholics.

It is significant that when Nietzesche taught at Basel, he had a painting of Holbein's Erasmus in his office. What did Nietzsche see by looking into Erasmus' eyes and soul?   Nietzsche's father was a Lutheran, and Nietzsche grew up in a pietistic Lutheran family (his father was a Lutheran minister). The protestant spirit lived in Nietzsche, but he carried the protesting tendencies a step further than Luther. Luther remained committed to his version of Lutheran Christianity. Nietzsche merely protested against Lutheranism and Christianity. Why be loyal to anything beyond protest?

My wife and I spent many a day at Sils Maria in the Engadine region of Switzerland where Nietzsche spent many a happy month in the 1880s. Some of Nietzsche's finest books were written in his room at Sils near the spacious rock fortresses in the area. My wife and I walked the Fex Valley where Nietzsche often walked and did the Nietzsche trek from the back of his flat at Sils. The point to note here, though, is that Nietzsche carried the idea of protest to the point where he opposed and left behind Christianity---loyalty was trumped by critical questioning and the lone and isolated critic came to dominate the day. Did Nietzsche see in Holbein's Erasmus the path he would take by following Luther yet further down the protestant path? Nietzsche or Erasmus? I spent many an hour in the home where Nietzsche wrote some of his finest books and pondered the relationship between Erasmus- Luther, Luther-Nietzsche and Erasmus-Luther. History was unfolding before my eyes in the very places where decisions were made to move the West further down the protesting path. There remains, in the interpretation of Nietzsche, questions about his relationship to Christendom, Christianity and Christ. Nietzsche was, in many ways, faithful to the underlying principles of both Luther and Protestantism.

Martin Heidegger wrote four books on Nietzsche, and although he taught most of his life in Freiburg, his real philosophic and contemplative home was his hut in Todtnauberg in the Black Forest in Southern Germany. My wife and I took the journey to Heidegger's Hut in Todtnauberg, and we did the Heidegger tour (rundweg) when in Todtnauberg. I slipped down to Heidegger's Hut where he wrote most of his books that shook and challenged most of western rationalist philosophy and theology. There is no doubt that Heidegger was a mystic in search of a deeper, more contemplative, more receptive way of knowing and being. His interest in the Orient (Nietzsche also had this interest), Pre-Socratic philosophy and poetry speak much about an alternate way of doing philosophy, and the hut at Todtnauberg was certainly Heidegger's shrine and Delphic oracle. Luther protested against the Roman Catholic tradition and started (like most protestants) his own version and brand of Christianity. Nietzsche protested against Luther and Christianity and found in the Greeks and aspects of the East something that could slake his deeper thirst. Heidegger was more the mystic and contemplative than Nietzsche, but he protested against both Roman Catholicism and Protestantism and turned to the East, German poetry and the pre-Socratics for wisdom and insight. In short, the sensitive seekers of the post-catholic and post protestant protesting tradition used the very protestant notion of protest to distance themselves from Christendom, Christianity and Christ. The notion of protest-loyalty that Erasmus had held so high had been replaced by the simpler commitment to protest and rejection of the thing protested against. This did not mean, though, that the longing for something deeper would disappear and dissipate.

My final destination when in Europe was to visit Herman Hesse's home in Montagnola near Lugano. Hesse had spent time in Basel, and he had a great deal of affinity with some of Nietzsche's writings, but he was more conscious of being on an explicit spiritual search. Hesse, like Nietzsche, grew up in a pietistic protestant family, and he protested against such an upbringing. The turn against institutional religion by Hesse had much in common with Nietzsche and Heidegger. All three had thoroughly imbibed and internalized the protesting spirit of Luther (and those who followed him further down the protestant path). It does not take a great deal of reflection to watch the unravelling of Christianity with the coming to be of Protestantism. Nietzsche, Heidegger and Hesse stand very much in the tradition of Luther, but they carry the notion of protest further than Luther would have gone. But, it was Luther and lesser Protestants that opened the floodgate for protest contra loyalty.

Hesse lived in a conscious tension between a rejection of his protestant tradition, a passionate exploration of the East and yet a sentimental attachment to western Christianity. He died, in his early 80s, with a copy of Augustine's *Confessions* on his chest. It is 50 years this year since Hesse died (1962-2012), and many is the event in Europe that is being held to ponder the relevance of Hesse. There can be no doubt, though, that Hesse internalized the protesting tendencies of his family but used such a protest tradition to protest and reject his protestant and missionary upbringing. The protestant irony reaches its climax in those like Nietzsche, Heidegger and Hesse. Erasmus saw most clearly that once protest came to trump loyalty, loyalty to protest would be all that was left. The very tradition that Protestantism initiated eventually negated Protestantism:

Nietzsche, Heidegger and Hesse make this abundantly clear. This does not mean the deeper spiritual search for meaning has ended. Hesse, Heidegger and Nietzsche, in many ways, embody the end of Christianity and the turn to some combination of East and West for deeper wells to slake their soul thirst.

Most Protestants of the 16th century never could have imagined that the seeds they sowed in the field of history would have choked and destroyed the faith they held so near and dear. The clear-eyed Erasmus saw this all so well, hence his opposition to Luther and followers. My trip to the Black Forest in Germany and Switzerland brought yet greater clarity to why we need to turn to Erasmus and hear and heed what he has yet to say---this will be a real countercultural act---the modern and postmodern is just a matter of acting out a pre-ordained script of more and more splintering and fragmentation. In short, there is nothing prophetic or countercultural about holding high the flag of protest and further divisiveness-this is all quite trendy and the naïve will dutifully follow such a lead. But, Erasmus calls us to a more demanding way. Did Nietzsche see that back of Luther, Erasmus had much yet to say? It is by turning to this more classical and ancient way that a real turn can be made that goes much deeper in the culture wars that so beset us these days. Erasmus, indeed, has much to teach Nietzsche, Heidegger and Hesse about such a time tried path and way.

9

BURCKHARDT, NIETZSCHE, HESSE

Whose Version of Conservatism contra Modernity?

ermann Hesse mentioned, in the final paragraph of his "Foreward" to *If the War Goes On......*, a suggestive lead to understanding his life journey and a portal of sorts into those things that held him. And, I quote: "I must say: three strong influences, at work throughout my life, have made me what I am. These are the Christian and almost totally unnationalistic spirit of the home in which I grew up, the reading of the great Chinese thinkers, and the last not least, the work of the one historian to whom I have ever been devoted in confidence, veneration, and grateful emulation: Jakob Burckhardt".

Hermann Hesse, also, from his earliest writings, in an implicit and explicit way, to his final tome, *The Glass Bead Game*, grappled with the challenge and significance of Friedrich Nietzsche, Nietzsche being Fritz Tegularius in Hesse's final magnum opus just as Father Jacobus was Burckhardt. Nietzsche tends to be much more in the ascendant these days, whereas Hesse and Burckhardt have waned somewhat, but literal fashion shows come and go as do intellectual fashion shows. Hesse spent much of his life threading the needle between Burckhardt and Nietzsche and this essay will examine how he did this and, in the process, welcoming once again, Hesse and Burckhardt onto the stage of the broader public dialogue of the political good and how to think and live it.

It should be noted, at the outset, that Burckhardt (1818-1897), Nietzsche (1844-1900) and Hesse (1877-1962) were each and all suspicious of the emerging and aggressive political nationalism of Otto Von Bismarck (1815-1898) and Germany in the mid-late 19th century. The notion that a unified nationalism emanating from Berlin would shape and guide the future of Europe was an anathema of sorts to Burckhardt, Nietzsche and Hesse. This is why, in many ways, Burckhardt spent most of his mature days in Basel and, in time, Nietzsche (who was German, parted paths with Bismarckian German nationalism and taught in Basel with Burkhardt for almost a decade) and Hesse (being also German and Swiss) made Switzerland his home rather than Germany. The more decentralized and canton approach to politics in Switzerland, needless to say, ran counter to the centralized approach of Bismarck and the consolidated nationalism of Germany. But, there is much more to ponder about why Burckhardt, Nietzsche and Hesse challenged the drift and direction of European intellectual, cultural, spiritual, educational, economic, aesthetic and political history than merely the worrisome impact of Bismarck.

The highly secularized French revolution, rise of science, the significance of rationalism as a way being, secularism as an emerging ideology and a questioning of religion (in this case Christianity) were part and parcel of the emerging progressive liberalism of the time, Hegel being the prominent philosopher of dialectical progressivism. Who was questioning such an emergent liberal orthodoxy (which we call the modern project or modernity)? And, for those who deconstructed such a project, whose version and turn to history would be used as a diagnosis and prognosis? Burckhardt has often been misread and misunderstood but he was certainly on front stage in raising some pertinent questions.

Burckhardt was a virtual contemporary of Bismarck, Nietzsche was younger than Burckhardt (even though he imbibed significant aspects of the Burkhardtian distinction between three sources of authority: state, religion, culture (the latter being favoured and trumping the other two). Hesse grappled with the state, religion/spirituality, culture tensions in a way that Burckhardt did not and Nietzsche often excessively reacted against, pitting these three spheres of human experience against one another, culture often becoming, as with Matthew Arnold, the new religion. But, let us first discuss Burckhardt, ponder the Burckhardt-Nietzsche pro-contra, then Nietzsche-Hesse and conclude with Burckhardt-Hesse.

There are three fine PHD turned books on Burckhardt more than worth the reading as primers on Burckhardt and one book on Burckhardt of much fullness and significance: *Jacob Burckhardt and the Crises of Modernity*: PHD (2000), *Basel in the Age of Burckhardt: A Study in Unseasonable Ideas* (2000) and *Jacob Burckhardt's Social and Political Thought*: PHD (2004). It is, of course, best to actually read Burckhardt, but helicopter tours over the forest can offer a much-needed overview of a perspective by an important cultural thinker. There are, perhaps, five points to note in Burckhardt's thinking that made him a significant cultural historian. First, Burckhardt held high, as a civilizational and cultural model, the immense productive and creative output of classical Athens (more on this later) and Renaissance Italy. Second, he thought, with the coming to be of the modern notions of liberty and equality, a dimming and dumbing down of the deeper meaning and significance of creative individualism (that demanded of the creator effort and struggle) had been lost and sacrificed. Third, he thought that the collective violence of the French Revolution, that turned against the past and in a rational, calculating, utopian and violent manner naively assumed human willing would and could make history in a positive way, was a worrisome feature of modernity: past versus future, wisdom versus making, hierarchy of virtues and creativity versus equality of potential and output. Needless to say, the actions by the state in the French Revolution made him suspicious of an uncritical attitude towards the state. Fourth, Burckhardt's turning of the back, for the most part, on Christianity and an idealizing of Classical Athens-Renaissance Italy made for an either-or approach to western civilization. I should note, though, that Burckhardt's more reflective and contemplative read of western cultural history (and history reading us) made him, in many ways, sensitive to significant aspects of western and Christian history (although, by day's end, this was not his north star) — the conservative humanism of Burckhardt makes him a significant guide for many. Fifth, Burckhardt thought that with the coming to be of Socrates (and his excessively rationalist, logical and dialectical ways, the classical tragic Athenian way of "agon" (and the vital and creative struggle which is part of it) had lost its way by reducing culture and thought to logical arguments (rather than a vitalistic and creative aestheticism)---we can see the Apollonian and Dionysian either-or contrast at work in this analysis of the tensions in classical

Athens (whose version should be heeded and why?).

So, in sum, there are five building blocks to Burkhardt's vision of thought, arts, culture and civilization: 1) a certain read of classical Athenian and Renaissance Italy was pitted against modern liberalism and Christianity (Christianity being seen as a forerunner of modern democracy and liberalism), 2) liberal modernity (a sort of secularized Christianity) embodied the decline of the west into the "last man", 3) the French Revolution illuminated for Burckhardt where willing-power and the state, turning against the moderating wisdom of history, could turn and go—sheer violence under the guise of bringing into being a new utopian order was an anathema to Burckhardt---the powerful leader (Napoleon) who incarnated the *ubermensch* and *Gewaltmenschen* was an anathema to Burckhardt, 4) Burckhardt's more reflective, temperate and contemplative approach to history (even though he had his priorities about which periods of history he preferred) made him somewhat respectful about the role of Christianity within Western cultural history and 5) Socrates was seen as a problematic and unfortunate representative of the more complex Athenian way (birthing, in a certain manner, a simplified way of knowing—sheer rationalism—such rationalism and the way it has been admired by the west has led to the simplifying of ways of knowing, including the arts and culture). Let us now turn to Burckhardt and Nietzsche.

There have been four tendencies to be recognized when reflecting on the Burckhardt-Nietzsche relationship and such trajectories must be noted. Nietzsche was much younger than Burckhardt and when he came to teach in Basel in 1869 (where Burckhardt taught and where Nietzsche remained until 1879) Burckhardt was a much respected scholar and Nietzsche gave him the admiring nod (as he did the rest of his life, including in his final letter before having his breakdown). What, though, are the four schools of thought regarding Burckhardt-Nietzsche, where did both men walk the same path, where part company and why? First, there are those who see Burckhardt as an early and somewhat insignificant influence on the more significant Nietzsche, hence not worthy of more than a mention in the burgeoning Nietzsche scholarship and industry. Second, there are Burckhardt devotees who think Nietzsche thoroughly distorted, used, abused and misread Burckhardt's name and reputation to articulate ends that Burckhardt opposed and disclaimed. Third, there are those that argue that Nietzsche was the more creative and energetic thinker who anticipated the future (hence worthy of heeding) whereas Burckhardt was a reactionary conservative not worth the time reading or pondering other than his initial and superficial impact. Then, fourth, there are those (and such is the position I will take) that there were and remained many Burckhardtian insights that Nietzsche internalized, but there were, also, crossroads in the paths where they went in different directions. Such will be the next phase of this unfolding essay.

Where do Burckhardt and Nietzsche walk the same trail, where part paths and what difference does it make? First, Burckhardt and Nietzsche both argued that the modern liberal ethos led to a flattening out of human creativity, a reducing of human longing to the mediocre, a fragmenting of culture and a dimming of deeper human desire. Both men saw the reformation and enlightenment project, with their progressive and optimistic notion of human nature, as naïve and a pandering to mass consumption. Needless to say, this made them, at one level, seemingly conservative reactionaries against the modern liberal notion of the superficial self. Interestingly enough, both held high the place of the creative individual, classical Athens and renaissance Italy their models, and the intense creativity of such moments in history soared beyond the pale creativity of their age and ethos.

Second, both men took the position that classical Athens, at its best, was not about a culture, through analytical reason, bringing into being the harmonious and good life. In fact, classical Athens embodied, in thought and deed, an understanding of the deeper tragic nature of reality, how to both live and create with such a perception and suspicion of reason as means to answer life's troubling questions. Both men thought Socrates birthed such a problematic way of being and, sadly so, gave the west a questionable silver bullet to solve the social and political journey of the all too human journey. In short, both men were suspicious and cynical about reason delivering the goods in any sort of meaningful or comprehensive manner.

Third, there was a tendency by both men in what might be called their trichotomy to elevate culture above what might be interpreted as the more oppressive aspects of the state and religion. This means that the realm of the social principle and culture were seen as that which lifted life to a higher level than the more moderate and constrictive aspects of the political principle (state) and religious principle (church). Both men did realize, though, that it was, often, the state (political principle) and religion (church) that supported some of the most significant works of creative culture in western civilization, so when interpreting Burckhardt and Nietzsche it is important not to push the trichotomy in a direction that only collides and is in conflict.

Fourth, both men, when they thought about and interpreted Christianity, tended to lean towards the more classical, catholic and pre-reformation forms of Christianity. This does not mean, though, catholic Christianity was where they finally took their leads and cultural cues.

Fifth, both men were suspicious of the emerging bourgeois and entrepreneurial west, the nouveau riche, a parvenu ethos and those who had no significant sense of culture and the arts. And, sixth, both men quaffed from the well of the *ubermensch*, hence very much artistic aristocrats even though their understanding of the higher person meant the artistic political leader. The underlying notion of the overcomer, though, was very much predicated on the classical idea of the "*agon*" or struggle to reach ever higher levels of creativity and excellence. In short, hierarchy, overcoming and struggle made for a significant trinity. But, where do such men part paths and why?

Burckhardt and Nietzsche had a particular commitment to the reading, interpretation and application of history. Those who linger for long with Burckhardt's *Reflections on History* and compare/contrast it with Nietzsche's *On the Advantage and Disadvantage of History for Life* cannot but be taken by master going in one direction and disciple in yet another direction. Both men had substantive questions and significant opposition to the use of history as a form of justifying aggressive nationalism and a form of approaching history in a detached and seemingly scientific and objective manner — this they could agree upon. But, Burckhardt's more nuanced, measured and judicious weighing of the tensions between, for example, the three powers of State, Religion and Culture (and the reciprocal action of the three powers) walks the reader to a different place on the historic terrain than Nietzsche's more reductionistic and, dare I say, ideological read of history (in which the reading and interpreting of history is "for Life" in the present tense). Burckhardt's read, yet once again, of "The Great Men of History" is layered and, in its own way, reciprocal, whereas Nietzsche's great men are leaning more in a similar direction. If both men are committed to the *ubermensch*, then the way they defined such a term was, often, at odds with one another. The great men for Nietzsche often, with their, *wille zu macht*, have worrisome tendencies towards the *Gewaltmenschen* (or more aggressive and violent means of overcoming and bringing into being a reality of self making and creating). The fact that Nietzsche had, in various places, not only fawned on Machiavelli but more importantly Machiavelli's nod to Caesar, Cesare Borgia and Napoleon, would make Burckhardt wince and shy away from the misuse and misdirection of power that, in places, Nietzsche seems to condone as a way of sweeping away the mediocrity of modern last men.

There can be no doubt that Burckhardt and Nietzsche opposed the disruptive and mercantile mentality that reduced all things to mobile commodities, and both men pondered how such a bourgeois and low culture ethos could be questioned and overcome, but Burckhardt, ever the classical humanist, thought that through education in the best that had been thought, said and done, fifth columns and ginger groups could offer an antidote to the toxins of the liberal modern way. Nietzsche was convinced that such a position was simply naïve given the run-a-way train of liberal modernity. Nietzsche thought that with the coming to be of the protestant reformation, enlightenment and secularism, such a delaying technique merely put a brake on the deeper nihilism that underlay the thin foundations of liberalism (with its sheer inability to articulate anything of nobility or of a higher virtue, ethic and ethos). It would just be a matter of time before the more thoughtful would deconstruct the paper thin core of liberalism and social and ethical confusion would occur (all choices being but fragile and untenable webs of meaning, meaning with no grounding or holding power). The reality of nihilism was always at the door awaiting the door and house to finally implode within and without.

There is a definite outworking of a political agenda that flows from the different philosophical and historical approaches of Burckhardt and Nietzsche. Both men were skeptical about liberal modernity in delivering on the goods, but they differed on how they might live within such a historic moment while being nourished by different reads of classical Athens and renaissance Italy. If democracy leads to a form of politics in which mass culture comes to shape and define the state, religion and culture, how are those to think and live who are committed to overcoming such low level and mediocre pandering to lowest level desires and trendy opinions? What does it mean to be an aristocrat of thought, culture and creative deed? Burckhardt realized, in some ways, the will to power that Nietzsche so justified was part of the modern problem, just a different version of it--- a more cultural rather than political (nationalism) or religious (religious wars and divisive denominations). The content of such merging of liberty and power was, obviously, different in politics and religion, but the notion of the dominance of liberty and power was something that all three powers shared. Burckhardt, ever the studious historian, saw only too keenly where this led and would lead in the cultural-political direction if Nietzsche took the throne (as he has for many)---liberty-willing facing into the abyss of nothingness and nihilism and a bringing into being, from chaos, ever different and at odds creative possibilities (many with dark and dangerous out workings).

Nietzsche often quoted and drew from Burckhardt as his model and mentor, but the more Nietzsche turned down an aggressive libertarian direction, the more Burckhardt (the conservative humanist of Basel) parted paths with him. Both men were convinced that history had to be more than antiquarian scholarship and only fit for museums---the best of the past, if rightly read and mined, could correct and redirect the problematic pathway being taken by liberal modernity. But, how many actually saw and understood the dilemma and its unfolding?—very few! They were like the perennial canaries in the mine shaft, the toxins of their times and implications of such toxins felt and internalized by them. Ideas do have consequences and some consequences take longer than others to bear their diverse fruit on the tree of such ideology. But, by days end Burckhardt and Nietzsche took different paths, Burckhardt being the faithful and loyal teacher in Basel, publishing less and less as he aged, his energy given more and more to public lectures and time spent with students. Nietzsche left Basel and took to Sils Maria in the Engadine Valley in Switzerland where some of his most powerful, challenging and pungent books were written before his early breakdown and death. How did Hermann Hesse find a middle way of sorts between Burckhardt and Nietzsche and why did he finally find more affinities with Burckhardt than Nietzsche?

There can be no doubt that Hesse did more than most, in his literary, religious and philosophical journey to make sense of the challenge of Nietzsche but, by day's end, it was Burckhardt that held him the nearest and dearest. How did Hesse engage Nietzsche, and what was it about Burckhardt that finally won the day, remembering, of course, that Burckhardt and Nietzsche both share a significant suspicion of the modern liberal project but they differ on how they both diagnose the problem and their prognosis in dealing with the illness. But, it is to Nietzsche and Hesse we now turn.

There are two poles or extremes from which Nietzsche's life and thinking tend to either polarize or dwell within an uneasy and trying tension. There is Nietzsche the destroyer, the model of deconstruction, the thinker with sword, hammer and fire in hand that exposes and undresses the no clothes emperor of metaphysics, religion, state, bourgeois society, positivist history and science, education, economics and seems to point the way to the cliff's edge of nihilism. It is from such a place that the weak despair, cynicism or skepticism take hold and a sort or paralysis occurs (or a retreat to the predictability and security of that which had been deconstructed). There seems, from one read of Nietzsche, the overcomer, the creative and strong souled ones who, from inner strength and self understanding, make themselves as a painter would paint on a blank canvass, a writer on a blank page. Such is one pole of Nietzsche, Nietzsche the courageous nihilist who brings meaning and purpose out of nothing or chaos. The other pole from which to read and interpret Nietzsche is his commitment to the notion of *amor fati* (love of one's fate). There is a sense, when read in a certain way, that the authentic overcomer merely overcomes what he/she have been conditioned to be but on the far side is the new being, the being yet waiting to be born, the being waiting upon and attentive to the daimon of fate (a sort of classical notion, in a way, of Lutheran grace)---all that is finite, conditioned, enculturated and fallible must be seen for what it is, including nihilism, and on the far side of such deconstruction is the Zarathustra prophet and harbinger of the new being who abides, heeds and loves the fate given to such an overcomer. Does then Nietzsche see a Zarathustra as one who also attempts to overcome fate itself (content of fate illusive and allusive) or love the givenness of fate? It is these two poles that Nietzsche often traverses in his thinking and prolific writing, his aphoristic probes and prophetic like pronouncements. How did Hesse, in heeding Nietzsche, heed the tendency towards deconstruction-nihilism on the one hand and *amor fati* on the other hand, Zarathustra, in many ways, Nietzsche's literary messianic figure?

Some of the earliest published writings of Hesse reflect and embody, in a searching yet somewhat immature manner, the unease that the sensitive artist in the world feels and is unsure what to do with: *Romantic Songs, An Hour Beyond Midnight* and a culmination of sorts, *The Posthumous Writings and Poems of Hermann Lauscher* (1901) reflect the mood and ways of the lone individual misunderstood and unheard in an unfeeling and uncaring world. There is an obvious sense that Hermann Lauscher has many an artistic affinity with both Nietzsche and Goethe's Werther, Lauscher the sensitive artist, at perpetual odds with the bourgeois and superficial world that he lives in, the gap between the comfortable, unquestioning, affluent bourgeois and the doubting, inwardly disoriented Lauscher inhabiting two different and, in many ways, external and internal realities. Hesse's early novels and prose did, for the most part, not sell well and such a reality, of course, reinforced within him the notion being the artistic outsider. It was, though, with the publication of *Peter Camenzind* (1904) that Hesse began to find his vocational way as a writer and artist. Peter is born into a small alpine village (isolated from the larger world), and his there and back again journey takes him into the larger urban, cultural and educational ethos in which the significance and cultural impact of Nietzsche reigns supreme both in an implicit and explicit way. Peter's journey takes him to the abyss a few times but his lingering time in Italy also exposes him to St. Francis of Assisi and Italian communities that live simply yet meaningfully. Peter could not dismiss them easily as a mindless herd. In fact, it is his participation and life with them that, in many ways, transforms him-- Francis, integration with community and serving of the least of these takes Peter to places he never anticipated---his final reconciliation with his father and return to the alpine vision he grew up in ends the novel. So, the question becomes, what is the content of the genuine overcomer? Is Zarathustra or Francis the way forward? Which decision, when standing over the abyss and nothingness should be chosen and why? Such were Hesse's initial probes into the challenge of Nietzsche.

The publication of *Under the Wheel* (1905) brought to the fore the clash between, this time, an authoritarian educational system and the sensitive creative artist, the educational system, like a steam roller, crushing the creative artist under its relentless wheel. Again, Hesse has an affinity with Nietzsche's many barbs against the German educational system of his time in which the true thinker and artist could be crushed by such a tank.

The pendulum swing between nihilism and *amor fati* heats up further and in a more demanding way in *Gertrude* (1910). The two dominant actors in this compelling novel take the tensions much deeper and further than the previous novels. Kuhn is a crippled composer who knows suffering, pain and inner anguish. It is, of course, somewhat understandable that he projects such erratic and senseless tragedy and unpredictability on nature and life in general--- how is it possible to affirm life when much of the evidence negates it? The other leading actor, Muoth, takes the nihilist path to one possible end—there is no meaning other than what we make, why bother making more creative meaning (all is transitory and an illusion), so suicide becomes Muoth's answer. Is this the path, Kuhn takes, though? Kuhn, by novel's end, dwells in the trying tension of nihilism leading to suicide, an unresolved, doubting and troubled faith in God and a rare blend of sensing the "divine within", a subtle *unio mystica* that is knit together with *amor fati*. Muoth embodies a direction nihilism can go and Kuhn takes a different direction, Hesse ever probing various ways to answer and massage Nietzsche and Zarathustra.

Needless to say, WWI revealed yet further paths possible to take on the nihilist path. The inevitable questions emerging from war about nationalism, brutality of war, destroying another person for the simple reason they are from another place across a border, human willfulness in mutual destruction, seeming silence from any transcendent reality pressed deep into Hesse's psyche. The fact his marriage was ending must not to be missed. The publication of *Demian* (1917) moves the Nietzschean overcomer to yet a more iconoclastic and sacrilegious position, Demian holding high Cain (killer of Abel) as a model of the strong and free versus the passive and weak Abel. The traditional father figure of God is jettisoned in favour of the complex Mother God Frau Eva. The naïve and maturing Sinclair is tutored into a different way of seeing and being by the more complex and challenging Demian, nihilism flirted with but layered Jungian archetypes merging and mingling in the mind and imaginations of Demian and Sinclair, Jung himself having written much on Nietzsche, Hesse being a patient of both a Jungian counsellor and Jung himself. There can be no doubt that *Demian* is a novel not to miss in Hesse's ongoing journey with Nietzsche and ways of engaging him. It is significant to note as

WWI came to an inevitable end, Hesse published his lengthy and not to be missed *Zarathustra's Return* (1919). *Zarathustra's Return* is Hesse taking up the mantle of Nietzsche and using Nietzsche's Zarathustra metaphor as a way of debunking and opposing the German spirit of aggressive hawkishness in a way that Nietzsche's notion of the *ubermensch* could not be confused or equated with--the herd mentality of German nationalism, in short, was anti-Zarathustrian. Hesse's use of Zarathustra both made it clear that Hesse was indebted to Nietzsche but his interpretation of Nietzsche clearly separated Nietzsche from those (such as Nietzsche's sister) who attempted to use Nietzsche to prop up and legitimate German fascism and Nazism.

There is, of course, Hesse's ongoing interaction with Nietzsche in most of his novels, but it would be remiss to miss his equally significant engagement with Dostoevsky in his two articles, published in 1920, in his book, *Glimpse into Chaos*. *Glimpse into Chaos* has two poignant and not to be missed essays on two of Dostoevsky's novels, *The Brothers Karamazov* and *The Idiot*. The subtitle of the essays is appropriately entitled "The Downfall of Europe". Hesse, like most sensitive thinkers in the late 19th and early 20th centuries, realized Europe was quickly losing its ethical, metaphysical and religious mooring. WWI only revealed the sheer emptiness and vacuity of a core and north star by which Europe might orient and chart its future. The notions of liberty sans content and laissez-faire identity and ethics meant any sort of meaning could be made by the willing individual. Hesse probed such a worrisome nihilism in the Russian novels mentioned above and his notion of the emerging "Russian Man" was, in many ways, the stark opposition of the more classical and humanist notion of the *Homo sapiens* (a common humanity grounded in a desire to live into wisdom and from such a centered place). Hesse suggested in his two essays on Dostoevsky's novels that the emerging nihilism would produce men and women that opposed any sort of restraint in the name of freedom and liberty and, in the process, would inevitably lead to the downfall of Europe. Hesse even suggests, in these essays, that "it seems to me that European and especially German youth are destined to find their greatest writer in Dostoevsky — not in Goethe, not even in Nietzsche". Needless to say, Hesse focussed on that part of Dostoevsky's novels in which the main protagonists had turned against any restrictions, forms and obstacles and asserted their wants, wills and a making and defining of reality in any shape, colour and size they wished. There is, of course, the deeply religious Dostoevsky who opposed such a drift and direction but the opposite pole was the Russian Zarathustras. Hesse, in his two essays, probes and bores into the emerging ethical and metaphysical vacuum and malaise in Europe post-WWI, in some ways, *Demian* was his initial literary attempt to face into the challenges of both Nietzsche and Dostoevsky.

There is an obvious turn in Hesse's writing after *Demian* and *Zarathustra's Return* to a deeper spirituality in *Siddhartha* (1919-1922). Siddhartha is wary of Gotama the Buddha and much of his journey is more about learning to live into and from love, the pain and suffering of love, and the redemptive nature of love. Siddhartha, by novel's end, becomes the kindly and wise ferryman who takes pilgrims from the shoreline of what they are leaving behind, across the waters to the shoreline of where they are going. There is an emerging depth in *Siddhartha* that has some affinities with St. Francis and Peter Camenzind. Who then is the real overcomer and *ubermensch*? There is no doubt that Siddhartha goes to places of insight and wisdom that Demian, Sinclair, Kuhn and Muoth do not. What does it mean, therefore, to become the new being and how is Hesse parting with Nietzsche in such a read and approach, the actual content of the overcomer seeming at odds with one another.

The shift from a seemingly deeper, simpler and more integrated notion of the spiritual overcomer in *Siddhartha* gave way to Hesse's more frayed and divided notion of the human soul in *Steppenwolf* (1927). Harry Haller, the main protagonist in the novel, is a divided person, part a wild wolf of the steppes, part drawn to the urban, civilized and cultured world of the city. There can be no doubt Harry despises the petty and bland ethos of the bourgeois last man, the middle class herd person who neither thinks nor feels deeply. Harry, like previous protagonists, sees much of social and human reality as a construct, the language and practice of good and evil being a means the weaker use to protect themselves from the demands of the stronger, the more passionate, the more in touch and in tune with their inner and deeper *amor fati*.

There are many affinities in style and content between *Demian* and *Steppenwolf*, Nietzsche's Zarathustra ever being pondered, worked through and evaluated. Martin Buber, in his fine article on Hesse ("Hermann Hesse's Service to the Spirit") for Hesse's 80th birthday, in *A Believing Humanism: My Testament 1902-1965* (1967) rightly so, I think, hinted at the dilemma within Hesse's literary struggles. There seemed to be two trajectories Hesse was going in his interaction with Nietzsche. Hesse could continue the path of the vitalistic, artistic, maker of history who, again and again, alone and lonely, isolated yet refusing to conform, misunderstood by nation, state, community and middle class, standing over the abyss of nihilism, through sheer force of will, overcomes the emptiness within and without, skepticism and cynicism of the weaker willed ones. Or, Hesse could ponder yet deeper and further a more significant and substantive notion of meaningful overcoming that was grounded in the demands of community and service to a fuller good. Such, in some ways, was the bent and direction of *Narcissus and Goldmund* (1930).

There is an obvious sense in *Narcissus and Goldmund* that Goldmund remains, in a variety of ways, the uber artistic individualist who indulges both physical and creative appetites to the fullest measure. Hesse does realize much is lost when the dynamic and engaged aspects of Narcissus are lost within the soul. It is, though, to Narcissus (most interesting how Hesse is redoing and rethinking this classical myth) that Hesse sees as the counterpoint---a probing of a deeper communal spirituality, somewhat indebted to Siddhartha and Peter Camenzind, that Hesse explores in this maturing novel. It is, of course, not an either-or, but more a probing of the pro-contra of both Narcissus and Goldmund, the appeal of the liberty loving Goldmund (and the dangers of such notions of liberty) and the more ordered, disciplined and communal artistic/monastic vision of Narcissus that keep this novel in living tension. There can be little doubt, though, that the issue of the conditions for authentic freedom is being pondered in this transition novel. I think it can be legitimately argued that Goldmund seems to be the more attractive actor on the stage, but Narcissus is about to emerge as a serious option and contender to Zarathustra.

There is a sense in *The Journey to the East* (1932) that Hesse has made a definitive turn in his understanding of the overcomer. What within and without is meant to be overcome? I have covered, in previous essays, the content and core of *The Journey to the East* (refer to these articles) but suffice it to say that Leo in *The Journey to the East* is the regal, royal, mature overcomer who is the head of the spiritual League of those travelling to greater depths (both past and present). Leo is also the hidden (throughout most of the novel) servant of all servants, Leo himself being Francis of Assisi's dearest friend, the metaphor of Leo the lion being one who has disciplined desires for a higher spiritual good (important to recall at this point Zarathurstra's three phases of transformation, the lion being the second). Leo is, in many ways, a more mature and deeper version of Narcissus, Siddhartha and Peter Camenzind. So, the deeper and more perennial question becomes this: whose version and vision of the overcomer is the most convincing and why? Hesse was very much moving in the direction of the classical humanist, Nietzsche was veering off in another direction. There is a succinct summary of Leo's position near the end of chapter 1 in *The Journey to the East* and I quote from it. Leo has been commenting on how both mothers and artists abiding appeal is the way they give birth to and serve both children and artistic creation — at times, the mother and artist seem weary and worn low in the doing of the deed and being true to such a fate. And yet, Leo has this to say:

"Perhaps it is sad and yet also beautiful. The law ordains that it shall be so"

"The Law" I asked curiously, "What law is that, Leo?"

"The law of service. He who wishes to live long must serve, but he who wishes to rule does not live long".

THERE is an obvious position being taken by Leo, those who know and are willing to serve their inner vision, spark, fire, and fate produce life and life abundant but this only occurs through self understanding and serving-birthing-being a midwife of that which is deepest within and most responsible without. The two German words, *knecht* and *dienst* are essential to understand in Hesse's approach and response to Nietzsche.

Let us now turn to Hesse's final answer and synthesis in his response to Nietzsche in *The Glass Bead Game* (1943). There are six things to note in approaching *The Glass Bead Game.* First, the full-bodied tome is "dedicated to the Journeyers to the East", hence the earlier book, *The Journey to the East* is a must-read entrée and portal to *The Glass Bead Game.* Second, Joseph Knecht is the main protagonist in the book and it is his life, reflections and journey that are front and centre---he becomes Magister Ludi (and all the complications and crises of conscience this brings him), but the names given him by Hesse are significant. Third, Knecht is both the German word to serve and etymologically it is the cognate of the English word Knight. Hesse is suggesting the real knight, the one who struggles and fights for the good, true and beautiful is not a well trained military person but one who struggles to unite the highest cultural visions of the past and present (such is the vocation of the Castalians who play the glass bead game). Fourth, Joseph is also connected to the Biblical Joseph (who served at the highest levels in the Egyptian court) and, interestingly enough, Thomas Mann's trilogy on the perennial yet Jewish Joseph (published before *The Glass Bead Game*). Fifth, both Burckhardt and Nietzsche factor significant in *The Glass Bead Game*, although Burckhardt (Father Jacobus) is much more a substantive core and main actor than the more erratic yet brilliant Nietzsche (Fritz Tegularius). Sixth, Hesse brings together, in a symphony of sorts (music and harmony being a foundational metaphor for the Castalians), his final vision in this book, his attempt to synthesize many of the trying tensions that beset those on the road to thinking and living an authentic life, contemplation and action (and an understanding of both) the foundation stones of his cathedral of thought and life, the Castalians the somewhat inadequate bearers of such cultural guardians.

My essay on *The Glass Bead Game* in this book should be read as an introductory reflection on this the final, fullest and ripest vision of Hesse (who won the Nobel Prize for Literature in 1946 for a lifetime or artistic and political activism). I would also encourage you to watch the three videos I did on *The Glass Bead Game* for an oral and visual synopsis of the magisterial tome (Clarion Journal: April 11 & April 29 2017).

I began this article by suggesting that Burckhardt and Nietzsche were two formative influences on Hesse's life and writings and yet, at the deepest level, as mentioned in the introductory quote, Burckhardt was the more informative. What was it about Burckhardt that took Hesse to places that Nietzsche was incapable (in his oft reactionary ways) of doing? I will conclude this missive by highlighting five areas in which Hesse had greater affinities with Burckhardt than Nietzsche.

There can be no doubt that Burckhardt, Nietzsche and Hesse were on the same page in questioning the crass nationalism and crude statism of their age and ethos. They also had little patience for the emerging entrepreneurial culture of the bourgeois philistine class that measured all on the transient scales of profit and loss, the primacy of Culture one of the first victims of such a dumbing down of that which makes the human quest of perennial significance. All three men shared substantive doubts about the project of liberal modernity, their aristocratic notions of the primacy of Culture being an affront to equalitarian modern thought and culture, but paths do part. Hesse and Burckhardt, in their perspectives, trek different trails than Nietzsche. There are five differences I will lightly land on.

First, Hesse and Burckhardt did their thinking in a more measured and irenical manner, carefully weighing the best that had been thought, said and done at the high points of the past, absorbing such insights and passing them on through their publications and teaching. Nietzsche tended to be more confrontational, doing philosophy with a sledge hammer (in this sense, very much like Luther). Burckhardt and Hesse were more like physicians of culture, doing their cultural operation with the finesse and nuancing of a surgical knife. So, the very method of thinking is quite different---the one irenical the other confrontational.

Second, Burckhardt and Hesse had a greater sensitivity to the layered and complex role of spirituality and religion than Nietzsche (who tended, once again, to fire hose Christianity, even though he could be more sensitive to the Roman Catholic than the Protestant tradition). Hesse was, I might add, much more probing and sensitive to religion and spirituality than Burckhardt (who was interested in religion as a historic phenomenon but kept an academic and personal distance from it in reality). Hesse's ever deeper interest in the contemplative aspects of religion and spirituality are most obvious in such novels as *Siddhartha, Narcissus and Goldman, The Journey to the East* and *The Glass Bead Game*.

Third, the fact Hesse had a much greater interest in spirituality and religion means Burckhardt's trilogy of State, Religion and

Culture (in which Culture took the lead) was more complex in Hesse (who thought the dialogue and interaction between Culture and Religion was more significant than Burckhardt and Nietzsche were willing to grant).

Fourth, Burckhardt and Hesse did, in many ways, embody in their commitment to place (Burckhardt in Basel, Hesse in Montagnola) the notion that the local and small is beautiful politics the best and finest way to live their public lives, Switzerland (with its many cantons) embodying such a political way of being.

Fifth, Hesse was less enamoured by classical Athens and Renaissance Italy than Burckhardt and Nietzsche. The noble and great men within aspects of these moments of cultural renewal held Hesse less. Hesse had a greater and grander sense of both comparative literature and civilizations, but more important yet, his notion of greatness was measured by the quiet and often ignored virtue of those who serve and are generous to others: Jesus, western and eastern monks and holy people, Francis of Assisi, Peter Camenzind, Narcissus, Leo and Joseph Knecht are models that Hesse turns to as the north star, the German words of *knecht* and *dienst* portals into Hesse's vision in a way that are foreign to Burckhardt and Nietzsche's notion of the makers and shapers of history. I might add, though, that Burckhardt did give the nod to the ascetics in the early church, that does need to be recognized but many of his great men of history are quite different as Cultural ikons—Hesse does nudge Burckhardt further in the direction he had some affinities with.

It is time to thread this essay to a close. In sum, Hesse was substantively impacted by Burckhardt and Nietzsche but it was Burckhardt that did more than Nietzsche in shaping his thinking and life. This did not mean, though, that Hesse swallowed Burckhardt whole. There are many significant ways in which Hesse took a bend in the trail (and such a different trail taken took him to unique sights and landscapes) and it is to such places seen and lived within that Hesse's unique vision and attractive qualities make him of perennial interest. It is, though, Hesse's blending of a grander religious synthesis, shaped and defined by service (*knecht-dienst*) within an inner self understanding of *amor fati* and the *unio mystica* that takes him to places Burckhardt and Nietzsche do not go. And, Burckhardt, Nietzsche and Hesse bring to us, given their mining of the western direction (and the challenge to it these days), this simple question and answer: whose version of the western (and eastern) tradition should be heeded, heard and why? Hesse, it seems to me, offers the better and fuller, more nuanced and insightful, the deeper humanist and classical approach that transcends time and place yet is perennially applicable to both.

APPENDIX
Knecht and Dienst: A Probe

ermann Hesse, in the "Foreward" to the 1946 edition of *If the War Goes On*.... mentions that "three strong influences, at work, throughout my life, have made me what I am". He then lightly lands on such influences: his Swabian German pietistic upbringing, Chinese thinkers, and Jakob Burkhardt. What might bind together such influences that made Hesse "what I am?" Perhaps, such a hint and pointer might be found in Book I of *The Journey to the East.*

The narrator in *The Journey to the East* has been part of a significant group called "The League". The League is a conscious group of spiritual thinkers that have drawn together the best that has been thought, said and done in the history of the human journey into a grand synthesis of insight and wisdom. Each and all in the League are committed to, in a personal and communal way, understanding and living forth the wisdom and meaning of such insights. What, though, might be the core and centre of such an abiding vision?

The narrator in Book I encounters Leo who seems, at first glance, to be the servant and Sherpa of the league. Leo packs up the bags for the pilgrims, brings their food, does their dishes, carries the bulk of their belongings (and much else) that eases the material needs of those on the quest. Leo, for all intents and purposes, seems to be the hired hand for those with deeper, grander and greater spiritual commitments and longings. And yet? And yet? There is a telling conversation between Leo and the narrator that is a portal into Hesse core vision. Leo suggests that there is a law or structure at the heart of things that we ignore to our peril and those on the quest for meaning and life must learn it. What is such a law?

> "The Law?" I asked curiously. "What law is that, Leo?"
> "The Law of service. He who wishes to live long must serve, but
> He who wishes to rule does not live long"

THERE is much compressed into this compact and not to be forgotten insight of Leo, and such an insight can be found in much of Hesse's writings as a counterpoint to other options. Most of Hesse's more mature short stories and novels probe, ever further and deeper, the diverse nature of the human soul, paths to take as a means of fulfillment, meaning and purpose and consequences of such choices. Some of the darker and more ominous novels such as *Demian* and *Steppenwolf* are more about indulging various appetites and desires, speculations and possibilities of life, much being liquid and fluid, willing wishes and living from such willed wishes. There is a sense in which *Demian* and *Steppenwolf* are must reads for the simple reason that inner and willed exploration (and the individual freedom to indulge such a journey) is at the heart and core of the authentic life. But, is this Hesse's final word or merely a phase that, by day's end, is a cliff's edge and cul-de-sac? And, what might Hesse-Leo mean by the law of service?

Hesse had a tender and probing mind and heart and his notion of the law of service had a core and radiated ever outwards. First, the inner law of service had much to do with serving, being attentive to and heeding the deeper inner life, and being part of birthing the real self rather than pandering to the inflated wants of the imposter ego (and its multiple addictions and erratic choices). It was in this attentive listening and responding to the inner depths (and living from such a place) that the ego could be seen for what it was and a more meaningful life might be lived. This is why, although Hesse explored a variety of identity options, he realized many were rabbit trails. Second, if the law of service was, initially, meant to be one in which the self was properly birthed, matured and grown, so service was meant to be front and centre in the communal human journey also. If, in short, the spiritual and religious quest bypassed service, the quest was an opiate of sorts.

We can see, in Hesse's novels, short stories and much else, those who seem to be overcoming the bourgeois and philistine way of life, in fact, are only reacting to it and, in reality, gorging the ego. So, what seems to be an overcoming is, in fact, a being caged by the ego. All this is so subtle and yet so real, the overcoming not a deeper overcoming. The real overcoming is when the self-overcomes the demands of the ego and this is best illuminated by the discipline of service and care for the self and others (at a variety of levels). We can see this worked out in most of Hesse's novels: Peter's turn to St. Francis, Siddhartha, Narcissus, Leo and Joseph Knecht but echoing the same motif. It is significant to note that, in Greek myth, Narcissus (from which we get the narcissistic personality) is seen as a place not to go. The longing of Narcissus, of course, is the desire to know true identity — needless to say, the shallow surface of the water is not the place to look — only a surface reflection is returned as the answer. But, Hesse realized that the longing of Narcissus is legitimate, the places gone to are the problem. Hence in his superb novel, *Narcissus and Goldmund,* Hesse highlights the nature of proper and genuine self-love and other love (community being the context within which such a reality is lived forth). The more Hesse's pondering and reflections matured, the more he moved from the lone individual searching for a meaningful identity (in all sorts of convoluted and complex ways) to the role of persons in community and how community and personhood are, when properly understood, a hand and glove fit.

Narcissus and Goldmund, The Journey to the East and *The Glass Bead Game* embody and reflect Hesse's notion of service within the context of community. Joseph Knecht, magister of the glass bead game, means the one who serves, *knecht*, in German meaning servant — the word also overlaps with the English word for knight (again, one who, serves).

Leo is servant of all servants yet he is the leader of the League. There are two words in German that embody layered ways of understanding the meaning of servanthood (*Knecht* and *Dienst)* and throughout most of Hesse's novel's, he is ever massaging the meaning of the words at a personal and political level. In sum, therefore, the golden key that will open the door into Hesse's novels and life is the key of the law of service and Hesse, again and again, returns to this core theme in his writings and life. If, therefore, we are to understand Hesse, we must return to such a persistent theme and be attentive to how Hesse understands it. I might add, then, by way of conclusion, that what Hesse's German Swabian pietistic upbringing, his interest in Chinese thinkers and Burckhardt shared in common was an understanding of service as the portal into life and life abundant.

Made in the USA
Monee, IL
13 September 2021

77927518R00094